The 21st Century
ENTREPRENEUR

HOW TO START
A SERVICE BUSINESS

The 21st Century

ENTREPRENEUR

HOW TO START A SERVICE BUSINESS

BEN CHANT
and
MELISSA MORGAN

A Third Millennium Press Book

AVON BOOKS  NEW YORK

THE 21ST CENTURY ENTREPRENEUR: HOW TO START A SERVICE BUSINESS is an original publication of Avon Books. This work has never before appeared in book form.

AVON BOOKS
A division of
The Hearst Corporation
1350 Avenue of the Americas
New York, New York 10019

Copyright © 1994 by Third Millennium Press, Inc., Stephen Pollan, Ben Chant and Melissa Morgan
Published by arrangement with the authors
Library of Congress Catalog Card Number: 93-50859
ISBN: 0-380-77077-6

Library of Congress Cataloging in Publication Data:
Chant, Ben.
    The 21st century entrepreneur : how to start a service business / Ben Chant and Melissa Morgan.
        p. cm.
Includes index.
1. Entrepreneurship—United States. 2. Service industries—United States. 3. New business enterprises—United States. 4. Success in business—United States. I. Morgan, Melissa, 1962–   II. Title.   III. Title: Twenty-first century entrepreneur.
HB615.C575 1994   93-50859
658.1´141—dc20   CIP

First Avon Books Trade Printing: August 1994

AVON TRADEMARK REG. U.S. PAT. OFF. AND IN OTHER COUNTRIES, MARCA REGISTRADA, HECHO EN U.S.A.

Printed in the U.S.A.

OPM 10 9 8 7 6 5 4 3

Thanks to Stephen Pollan and
Mark Levine for their guidance and patience

⇜ **CONTENTS** ⇝

The 21st Century

ENTREPRENEUR

HOW TO START A SERVICE BUSINESS

I.
As Simple As ABC

The first part of our book answers these basic questions: Why should you start a service business? Will you be a good 21st Century entrepreneur? And how do you pinpoint a successful idea?

⋙ 1 ⋘
HOW TO USE THIS BOOK

Service in the 21st Century

Yes, you should start a service business—a business, such as a law firm or a fan club, that has a service as its product—and you should do it now. Ever since the end of World War II, retailers have been scrambling after ever scarcer customers, and manufacturers have found themselves crippled by high start-up and labor costs, while service businesses have been growing faster than any other segment of the economy . . . and that's been true in both economic booms and busts. Service businesses generally have lower start-up costs than other types of businesses, making them the ideal choice for entrepreneurs with a limited budget. And count on it—service businesses will be the most successful businesses of the 21st Century.

While the dawn of the new millennium is really nothing more than a date on Pope Gregory's calendar, it does lend an air of importance to a revolution that's going on right now: the information revolution. Just as the printing press changed the lives of those living in the late fifteenth century, so the rapid proliferation of information will continue to alter our lives. We already live at a more frenetic pace than our parents, who lived faster than our grandparents.

What society needs are businesses that can make this new pace manageable. In one form or another, that's what most service businesses do, whether they are express mail companies, law firms, or home-cleaning outfits. While the groundwork for this revolution has been laid for the past twenty years, it's in the next decade that these new businesses will flourish. People, like you, who start their service businesses right now—just as the revolution really kicks in—will be able to profit tremendously in the coming years.

That doesn't mean starting a service business today will be a piece of cake. There are a number of fundamental changes and problems 21st Century entrepreneurs such as you will face, issues we'll be returning to often in the course of this book.

The first problem is potential obsolescence. Because the pace of life is moving faster and faster, your company must be able to make rapid changes if it's to keep ahead of the pack. You can't set up a business and expect to do the same thing until you retire. Circumstances, market forces, and clients will be forever changing from now on. Unless you've prepared for this constant change, your business will be left behind and you'll be left wondering what went wrong. Here's where the small size of your company is a great advantage: You'll be able to adapt and change much faster than a large company. While they are all still floundering, wondering how to relate what they do to the new needs of their customers, you'll be able to turn on a dime.

Another problem for entrepreneurs, even those running service businesses, is that in the future there will be more competition for customers. If you're reading this in the bookstore, just take a glance over your shoulder. There are probably at least two other people browsing through the "how to start a business" section along with you. Those are two potential competitors. You should be concerned, but not worried. We will show you how to beat those two rivals, and any others, by making your company unique and knowing exactly what your customer wants . . . even before he or she asks for it.

You need to understand that successful companies in the 21st Century aren't going to make money simply by charging a high price. Profit in the future will be the result of careful planning and steady growth. That will require a well-thought-out idea, a wariness of taking on too much debt, and an omnipresent cash cushion in case of another recession. (If the recent recession did nothing else, it proved that the Reagan Era concept of an ever-expanding economy was dead wrong. It's a sure bet there will be both booms and busts in our economic future.) It also means you'll need to concentrate on your core business and develop it cautiously, being ready to adapt and change as need dictates, but without making impulsive decisions. And once you're set up, you'll need to plan even further into the future for eventual expansion and evolution.

You probably already have a hunch that running a service business is what you ought to do. Why else would you be reading this book? Maybe you've even started to research your ideas. This book will show you how to go forward, how to turn your ideas and dreams and concepts into reality. But one word of advice: Act quickly. You need a sense of urgency. Every day, new businesses are being registered down at the town hall. You must move swiftly in order to take full advantage of your intuition, creativity, energy, and ideas.

You do have an ace in the hole: this book. It will give you an edge over existing and potential competition. The advice in this book was garnered from many experts and entrepreneurs. We've attempted to whittle away the fluff and provide you with only pointed and useful information. We've included only what applies to starting a service business, and we've updated a lot of old advice and ideas so they'll meet the needs of you: the 21st Century entrepreneur. By reexamining the old and discovering the new, we've written a road map to success. A road map that tells you, among other things, how to cope with the coming changes, how to decide which business to start, how to finance it, and, finally, how to develop it.

In a further attempt to cut through the information jungle and make your journey a successful one, we've written this book in plain English and have provided plenty of real-life examples to illustrate problems and solutions. We've paid special attention to the needs of readers who haven't had any experience running the financial side of a business. That's because we're convinced that no amount of creativity will compensate for a lack of financial acumen. And, while we're always encouraging, we also advise caution when necessary.

Each chapter in the book will explain one step in the process, leading you by the hand until you can make your own way. In Chapter Two we explore the advantages of starting a service business instead of a retailing or manufacturing business.

In Chapter Three we examine the personality of the successful entrepreneur. We've come up with a checklist of traits all the successful entrepreneurs we interviewed seem to have in common. By taking a simple quiz, you can see whether or not you have what it takes.

In the next group of chapters, Four, Five, and Six, we show how to develop an idea or refine one you already have. By identifying your interests and narrowing down the possibilities, we help you find a business that will both excite you and make you money.

With your idea fixed firmly in your mind, Chapter Seven helps you sort out the details of your new business. By using a new flexible checklist, we've transformed the traditional business plan into an easy-to-use document that can grow and change along with your company.

In Chapter Eight we discuss where you're going to locate your business, and look at the pros and cons of working from your home or from an outside office.

Chapters Nine through Eleven deal with money. This is, after all, a business you're starting, not a hobby. We'll show you how to calculate how much money you need to start up, how much you'll need to keep your business going, and where you can find it.

As you'll learn in chapters Twelve and Thirteen, it's no longer enough to advertise in traditional ways in traditional places. In these chapters we look at marketing and advertising in the 21st Century, showing how to use the old methods for whatever they're worth, and then demonstrating how to use your secret weapon: personal relationships with your clients.

Depending on the size of your company and how fast it grows, you may need extra help. In Chapter Fourteen we analyze the advantages and disadvantages of hiring people as either full-time employees or free-lancers. We'll also tell you how to attract and keep the best workers.

At that point you'll be ready to open for business. But we don't leave you out on a limb. That's because the entrepreneurial process isn't over when the door opens for customers. Chapter Fifteen tells you how to keep track of your finances. Like a shark, a business has to keep moving or it dies. The last two chapters,

Sixteen and Seventeen, show you why and when you should change or expand, and how to find the money to do so.

Despite all the advice we'll be providing in this book, we can't start the business for you. You must do it for yourself. Sure, there's a lot of hard work ahead of you, but we promise to prepare you for the difficulties you might encounter. It won't be easy, but the rewards, both personal and financial, can be great. With your own determination and perseverance, and our advice, you'll be able to combine business with pleasure and succeed as a 21st Century entrepreneur.

SMALL BUSINESS ASSOCIATIONS

The following are some of the many associations of and for small businesses. Where possible, we've included a telephone or fax number for you to call for more information. If no number is available, we suggest you speak with the reference librarian at your local library.

American Association for Consumer Benefits (AACB)

Promotes the availability of medical and other benefits to small business owners, their families, and employees. For information call (800) 872-8896.

American Small Businesses Association (ASBA)

Supports legislation favorable to the small business enterprise and organizes opposition to unfavorable legislation. For information call (800) 235-3298.

American Woman's Economic Development Corporation (AWED)

Provides extensive management training, on-site analysis of businesses, and support for women planning to start a business or who are already in business. For information call (800) 222-AWED.

Association of Small Business Development Centers (ASBDC)

Local centers providing advice, information, and advocacy for those planning to establish a small business.

Independent Small Business Employers of America (ISBE)

Works to assist members in keeping businesses profitable and maintaining good employee relations. For information call (800) 728-3187.

International Association of Business (IAB)

Keeps members informed of trends in the business industry and tries to secure for members benefits that are usually reserved for larger companies and corporations. For information fax (817) 467-0807.

International Association for Business Organizations (INAFBO)

Seeks to encourage and support international commerce among small businesses. Affiliated with National Association for Business Organizations, National Association of Home-Based Businesses, and Small Business Network.

International Council for Small Business (ICSB)

Promotes discussion of issues pertaining to the development and improvement of small business management. For information fax (314) 658-3897.

National Association for Business Organizations (NAFBO)

Represents the interests of small businesses to government and community organizations on small business affairs; monitors laws that affect small businesses; supplies members with marketing and management assistance; and encourages joint marketing services between members. Maintains the National Small Business Institute, which offers extension courses at affiliate colleges and universities for entrepreneurs.

National Association of Private Enterprise (NAPE)

Tries to ensure the continued growth of private enterprise through education, benefits programs, and legislation. For information call (800) 223-6273.

National Association for the Self-Employed (NASE)

Acts as a forum for the exchange of ideas and the promotion of political awareness. For information fax (800) 366-8329.

National Business Association (NBA)

Promotes and assists the growth and development of small businesses by aiding members in obtaining government small business and education loans, and making available insurance policies and software in conjunction with the U.S. Small Business Administration. For information call (800) 456-0440.

National Business Owners Association (NBOA)

Promotes the interests of small business by providing government relations services and member benefit programs. For information fax (301) 913-0001.

National Federation of Independent Business (NFIB)

Presents surveyed opinions of small and independent business to state and national legislative bodies through a fifty-person

legislative, research, and public affairs office in Washington, D.C.

National Small Business Benefits Association (NSBBA)

Offers discounts on group dental and life insurance, nationwide paging and travel programs, car rental, fax equipment, office supplies, and cellular phone services; and provides specialized services including business overhead analysis, management consulting, accounting services, marketing, public relations, and owner-to-owner networking. For information fax (217) 544-5816.

National Small Business United (NSBU)

Serves as administrative and legislative coordinator of Small Business Legislative Council (see separate entry). For information call (800) 345-6728.

Network of Small Businesses (NSB)

Aims to obtain expansion funding, new sources of supply, and low-cost cooperative advertising for members, who are primarily inventors, innovators, scientists, and engineers. Also offers health insurance programs, liability insurance funding, and loan assistance; provides legal advice and employee benefits counseling. For information fax (216) 449-3227.

Service Corps of Retired Executives Association (SCORE)

Volunteer program sponsored by U.S. Small Business Administration in which active and retired businessmen and businesswomen provide free management assistance to men and women who are considering starting a small business, encountering problems with their business, or expanding their business.

Small Business Assistance Center (SBAC)

A division of the Small Business Service Bureau that offers planning and strategy programs to aid businesspersons in starting, improving, or expanding small businesses.

Small Business Foundation of America (SBFA)

Charitable organization that raises funds for education and research on small businesses. For information fax (202) 872-8543.

Small Business Legislative Council (SBLC)

Permanent independent coalition of trade and professional associations that share a common commitment to the future of small business.

Small Business Network (SBN)

Provides management and marketing services, business evaluations, and import and export management services; and acts as umbrella group for: International Association for Business Organizations, National Association for Business Organizations, National Association of Home-Based Businesses, and National Small Business Institute.

Small Business Service Bureau (SBSB)

Provides national assistance with small business group insurance, cash flow, taxes, and management problems, as well as offering legislative advocacy, group benefit services, group insurance, and group health plans. For information fax (508) 791-4709.

Small Business Support Center Association (SBSCA)

Serves as a lobbying agent for small-business-related matters. Currently active only in Texas, the SBSCA plans to operate on a national scale.

Support Services Alliance (SSA)

Provides services and programs such as group purchasing discounts, legislative advocacy, and business and financial support services. For information call (800) 322-3920.

⤬ 2 ⤬

THE JOY OF SERVICE

Why You Should Start Your Own
Service Business Today

Deciding whether or not to start your own business is, in some ways, like deciding whether or not to have a child. Both require twenty-four-hour-a-day dedication, and both can bring you great joy.

We think the desire to be his own boss lurks in every American's heart: It's as American as the Grand Canyon and Presidents' Day sales. Napoleon disparaged the British as "a nation of shopkeepers." To Americans that would be a compliment. Have you ever walked down your local Main Street looking at the stores and found yourself thinking, "I could do that, and I could do it better"? You want to feel the pride and love that come from creating something that works, something that's done right.

Almost everyone has had the experience of working for someone else. We all know it can be a deadening experience. It shakes your confidence in your own ability. It makes you dependent on other people's whims. It inhibits your creative thoughts because you need to confer with others in order to get anything done. For at least eight hours a day, five days a week, the majority of Americans use their imagination and intelligence to make other people richer. And the sad fact is that the people being made richer are no more intelligent than their workers.

There's no substantive difference between you and your employer. The reason she's the boss and you're the employee is that someone whispered to her that she could do it. This book will be the voice in your ear that convinces you that you have what it takes to do what you want to do, to be your own boss.

Sure, you'll need to take risks. And yes, there is a possibility of failure. But let's get some perspective. We're talking about your life and how fulfilled it's going to be. As an entrepreneur, you'll make an interesting discovery: The money you make for yourself acquires a greater value than the dollar you earn for someone else. Your money develops a sort of spiritual value related to the pioneer ethic. The early pioneers placed great emphasis on self-reliance and the ability to provide for your family from the land. Nowadays, not many of us can afford (or even want) to become self-sufficient farmers and raise our own food. But owning your own business has the same satisfying effect. You attract a customer into the store, then watch as a dollar goes from the customer's hand into your till and is transformed into food for your family's table . . . or perhaps a new game cartridge for your son's Nintendo. Of course, various things—like the government and health insurance companies—will take hefty bites out of that dollar before it gets from the till to your table. But you'll still have the pleasure of knowing that you alone have provided for yourself or your nearest and dearest.

Surprisingly, one of the great advantages of starting your own business is that you get job security. You may need to close the entire business if something goes wrong, but you certainly aren't going to walk in one Friday morning and be asked to clear out your desk. And as we're sure most of you now realize, there is no longer any such thing as corporate loyalty out there in the business world. The recent corporate ''down-sizing'' has finally shown that the old notion of a paternal employer is nothing more than a cruel lie. In today's world you can show up on time, do your job well, and still get laid off. Employees are nothing more than expenses to 21st Century corporations.

As an entrepreneur, you'll find that financial independence can provide emotional security. Independence means you'll avoid the fear and concern that runs through a business when the employees aren't informed about major decisions. The tension generated by rumors about the financial health of a company can be exhausting and demoralizing. By running the business, you'll have the satisfaction and peace of mind of knowing the ins and outs of the finances. You'll know because you *are* the business.

Owning your own business gives you more flexibility, but it doesn't give you more free time. You could take vacations whenever you'd like. You could shut up shop early on a beautiful May afternoon. However, you'll find you won't actually do these things because you're working for the toughest boss in the world: yourself. You'll realize that every hour you spend goofing off is an hour you're not earning money. A free-lance writer friend of ours often goes to movie matinees because he hates to go to crowded movie theaters. "I hate crowds," he explains, "but I love movies, so I figure I owe it to myself to take advantage of the way my life is organized. Besides, there are great matinee discounts at my local cinema." But don't get the idea that this is an extended lunch break. We know that we can call him at his home office until midnight because he works late to compensate for his matinee habit.

You'll also find that owning your own business gives you a special kind of freedom—freedom of the mind. You won't need to answer to another person every time you choose to do something. You're making your own choices. These choices will be about everything from where to buy paper clips to whether or not you can afford to stay open for another month. But there's a flip side to this freedom of the mind.

In the course of researching this book, we've found there's nothing better than spending evenings in the company of entrepreneurs who keep business in perspective. These men and women are always full of good humor—for them, life has wonderful things to offer. On the other hand, an evening in the company of some entrepreneurs can stretch on forever. These are the people who experience the flip side to freedom of the mind: becoming obsessed with your business.

Don't get us wrong; as long as it doesn't destroy your personal life, there's nothing wrong with this obsession. Just make sure you stay in control of it.

WHY SHOULD YOU BE IN
A SERVICE BUSINESS?

There are two important reasons you should choose a service business over a manufacturing, wholesale, or retailing business: One is spiritual, the other is financial.

The category of "service business" includes many jobs, from tree surgeons to plastic surgeons. But what all service businesses have in common is interaction with others. You'll find service is the most people-oriented type of business. Service businesses touch people's lives and really make a difference. You're not going to become Mother Teresa, but you'll have more of a direct influence on the public than someone who owns an envelope-making factory. He'll never meet his customers; you'll go out of business if you don't know yours well and care about them.

The financial answer to the question "Why should you be in a service business?" is that service businesses are easier and less expensive to start up than manufacturing, wholesale, or retailing businesses. You'll be making enough of a leap of faith to just begin your small business. You want to make sure the river you jump over is as narrow as possible.

The beauty of the service industry lies in its very simplicity. You can get a grip on it.

A manufacturing business could be anything from three people making novelty watches in a garage to General Motors. However, whether you're GM or the watch maker, you have to deal with a slew of questions and problems: Where will the raw materials come from? Do you have your inventory under control? Who is going to do the work? Do you have enough space for your employees to do their work? Should you buy or lease your space and equipment? And you've got to answer all those before you even get a product to the market and find out whether or not your original idea was a good one.

A wholesaler performs a valuable task—passing on other people's products to the public—but it's hardly the stuff of entrepreneurial dreams. It's a business that takes a long time to learn: You need to know when and where to buy. You are, essentially, a warehouse manager passing along other people's products, constantly wondering whether you've bought too much of the wrong thing at too high a price.

Retailing is a more common option. In fact, a small store that gradually expands into a chain or franchise, à la Wal-Mart, is the classic entrepreneurial dream. Unfortunately, the image is flawed: We don't live in Mayberry anymore. The effort involved in discovering a consumer niche and a top-quality location may not be worth it. Sure, there will always be a place for a corner food market, but how many perfume boutiques, lighting fixture stores, and video outlets can one town support? There are always going to be niches that open up for imaginative retail store owners, but those niches are getting more and more specialized. We're reminded of the "Saturday Night Live" sketch in which the owners of a shop that sells only tape pace anxiously, waiting for someone to buy a roll or two.

In addition, most of us live in the suburbs. That makes a mall location essential for all but the most specialized retailer. And most malls are already carefully stocked with one of everything. Mall stores are often folksy fronts for big businesses that can beat out a small business in a price war in a matter of weeks—especially since the rent in the mall is so high.

A service business differs primarily because you're selling your expertise and time, not a product. Depending on your actual business, the consumer may have some physical proof of the service you've provided—a newsletter or a new mailing list, for example—but the customer may also leave with something intangible, like new information or ideas. This makes a service business ideal for the 21st Century entrepreneur because you can wake up in the morning and have an immediate grasp of your business. You don't need to worry about other people, and it's all yours to adapt and change as you desire. The recent recession was a temporary setback. But in general, Americans have more money to spend on whatever they like. And what they like is to have more time to do what they want. This is true for businesses as well as individuals. Experts disagree as to whether we have more or less leisure time, but everyone knows that we want to enjoy whatever time we do have.

A teacher we know said to us recently, "Why should I spend Saturday afternoon cleaning my house if I can afford to hire someone to do it for me? I can afford it. And shirts too; I hate doing those. I get home late and I'm exhausted. The last thing I want to do on a Monday is spend an hour and a half washing and ironing my shirts. It's worth it to me to send them out and pay someone else twelve dollars to do them. Not to mention the fact that they do a better job than I do!"

Both businesses and individuals will pay you to make their lives easier for them. Everyone prefers to do what interests them, what they do best, or what makes them the most money. You can make money by doing what they don't want to do, what they don't do well, or what they don't do profitably, but still needs to get done. One man's poison is another man's meat!

Experts predict that in the 21st Century nearly 90 percent of all jobs will be service-based. Almost half of these jobs will be geared towards some kind of information gathering or retrieval. The reason is that manufacturing has become a lot more efficient and less reliant on manpower. According to Sylvia Nasar, writing in the *New York Times,* "Virtually all of the 67 million new jobs created since World War II have sprouted in the services." Here are some other 21st Century trends, economy-related and otherwise, that offer golden opportunities for service-business entrepreneurs.

FILLING THE STAFF GAPS

"Streamlining and downsizing" is the euphemism companies are using when they are cutting back their entire operation. The reduction in profit and the unwillingness of their creditors to cut them any slack means they need to reduce their support staff in order to balance the books. The large corporations know it's cheaper to employ people part-time or with an official independent contract than it is to pay them full-time. Where there were once in-house lawyers, technicians, and public relations people, there are now outside firms brought in to do the work. By becoming one of these outside firms, you can make great profits. You can offer your services as a consultant, you can be a free-lancer, or you can work part-time.

FILLING THE SERVICE GAPS

Jobs aren't the only cutbacks that companies make. The range of products and services is also reduced. Some services are essential for a large business to offer their customers, yet they can be expensive. By taking over the task, you can cut their expenses and still allow them to offer their customers the same service. For example, a department store doesn't need to own its own fleet of trucks in order to deliver couches and wardrobes. An efficient independent contractor (you) can do the job just as well.

REPAIRING EXISTING PRODUCTS

A combination of the recession and the new concern about the environment is making people more open to repairing things rather than replacing them. The popular idea nowadays is that you should initially make a good, quality purchase and then repair it as needed, rather than throw it away and buy a new one. Let's take the example of a television. It takes valuable natural resources to make one. It makes no sense ecologically to throw it away and take up precious landfill space when it stops working. It does make sense that it should be cheaper to repair something than buy a new one. That's where the 21st Century entrepreneur can step in. Planned obsolescence is, thankfully, becoming obsolete.

DOING HOUSEHOLD CHORES

Another trend is that of families in which both parents work. This trend didn't begin with the recession, but the slow economy has led people to focus on the problems of having to rely on two incomes. These problems provide enormous opportunities for a new business. We talked earlier about people not having enough time for the run-of-the-mill tasks that must be done to keep their lives on track. Children or elderly parents make the situation even more complicated and provide opportunities for service businesses. There are plenty of services that these families need: looking after children and/or older people; doing the washing and ironing; dealing with bureaucracy; caring for pets; housecleaning; and food shopping. The markets for all of these services may have been sparked by the recent recession, but they'll continue to grow rapidly now and on into the next century.

OBTAINING AND PROCESSING INFORMATION

The recession has had an effect on the information revolution too. The avalanche of information available to consumers and businesses continued to gain momentum and increased in size, despite the fact that the economy was slowing down. This created a crisis for both individuals and companies. Businesses used to be able to afford departments to clip relevant articles and do background research. Now they are looking to outside people to do it. Where once they may have had the time and resources to make sense of the information on their own, now they need other people to sift through the information for them. They turn to data base companies and libraries that can provide information at the touch of a computer key and who have the expertise to preprocess the raw data and turn it into manageable reports. Having paid for such information processing, they are unlikely to go back to doing it on their own when the economy rebounds.

BRINGING ORDER OUT OF CHAOS

A whole new industry has already developed due to the need of businesses and consumers for help in dealing with the complexities of modern life. Paulette Ensign is one of the directors of the National Association of Professional Organizers. Talking about the individuals who make up the association, she says, "We have seen a tremendous growth. Nationally we have five hundred members. The more exposure we get, the more people say, 'Oh yeah! I can use that,' or 'Thank God you're around. When can you help us?' We run a very wide range of services, from closet and home organizing to corporate and individual business. Some organizers have even specialized and just deal with certain industries like law offices or medical offices and their health insurance claims. This service is being seen as less and less of a luxury and more of a necessity. People are making a choice, and more and more are willing to pay money to get their lives and businesses in order.''

TARGETING NICHE MARKETS

According to marketing analysts and sociologists, our society is becoming increasingly fragmented. The typical American family used to be fairly easy to define. Even though no real-life family could be that perfect, the Cleavers—Ward, June, Wally, and ''Beaver''—did represent the traditional makeup of households. Today, analysts have defined all sorts of groups that cut across family lines. There are, of course, the baby boomers and the tired yuppies. But there are also the dinks (double income no kids) and the aces (active college-educated seniors).

The proliferation of varied societal groups is great news for the 21st Century entrepreneur. Whereas a large company must market itself to many different groups in order to reach enough people to be profitable, the low overhead of a new entrepreneurial service business allows the owner to make a profit by focusing on a single, often very small, group. The entrepreneur can adapt his company and marketing strategy to the targeted group and eventually become invaluable to them. The larger, slow-moving company doesn't stand a chance.

PROVIDING BETTER SERVICE

Every family, regardless of which niche it may fit into, raised its expectations during the 1980s, even if it didn't really raise its standard of living. America wants its needs to be met quickly and efficiently, even if it can't afford top-quality items, and the old companies can't afford to offer top-quality customer service. This is where you'll step in. With your flexibility, low overhead, and willingness to listen to exactly what the customer wants, you'll steal customer after customer away from the less responsive established businesses.

All of these trends document one thing for certain: Society is changing. As it changes, you can be there to meet the new demands.

A service business is the way to succeed beyond the year 2000. And you'll do this by helping others to succeed at work and at home, and you'll charge them handsomely for it. You'll service their needs, and in doing so, fulfill two great needs in your own life: the creation of something worthwhile and, less selflessly, the need for money.

Plus you'll be helping to create a new society, just as Henry Ford did with the Model T and Steven Jobs did with Apple computers. The future isn't created by scientists at MIT or cartoonists working for Marvel Comics. No one lives in the sort of world envisioned by the cartoonists of the thirties, and no one will live in the kind of world today's visionary artists are drawing. Ordinary Americans like all of us will be the ones who create 21st Century America. Your company will be part of this new century, just as your children will.

And in this new world you and your new company will prosper. Probably.

In the next chapter, we'll examine one of the most important factors in a business's success: your personality.

⟨⟩ 3 ⟨⟩

WILL YOU BE A GOOD PARENT?

What It Takes to Be a 21st Century Entrepreneur

Being a parent has never been easy: Just ask your mother. Likewise, it's never been easy to start your own business. Because you want to be the best parent a fledgling company ever had, you'll need to know the personal qualities essential for success in the 21st Century. After talking with a number of business people from all over the country, we've isolated those character traits and experiences that seem to be present in most successful entrepreneurs. Don't worry, you don't need to have an abundance of all of them, but you do need some of each one. At the end of each section, we'll pose some lighthearted questions that will help you decide which of these personality traits you possess. As with so many quizzes of this type, it's obvious which answer is the best. But try not to cheat! At the end of each chapter we'll analyze your results.

In each quiz section, read the questions and then answer them honestly. Be realistic: It's better to know exactly which aspects of your personality will be assets and which will be liabilities to your company. The highest (4) and lowest (1) scores represent extremes, an emphatic yes or no. The middle scores (3) and (2) represent more moderate answers.

CONFIDENCE

This book, and the other research you do, will provide you with knowledge and tools, but most of the wisdom and skill has to come from you, much of it instinctively. You must radiate confidence—especially when you're asking people to invest their money in your business (although you'll need to beware of coming on too strong—no one likes to feel he's getting a hard sell). You must be confident when you meet your first client and make your first sale. You must be confident when you lose a client for the first time. And you'll need an awful lot of confidence to hire your first office manager when you expand.

Confidence has many other traits wrapped up inside it. There's resilience: the ability to bounce back from adversity. If you lose a major customer in the morning, make sure you call a potential client right afterwards and take him out to lunch. And make sure to order a decent bottle of wine.

That same confidence means you're comfortable taking smart risks. As it is, there's enough risk involved when you set up a business, so don't suddenly decide to expand into a new area without weighing the consequences: A calculated risk is okay, a wild gamble isn't. Sometimes the risks will be of a personal nature involving your ego; sometimes they'll involve cash. Whatever the nature of the risk, you'll need courage to take it.

And you can't spend time worrying about your ego; it has to get along on its own now. Just remember, a business rejection is a rejection of your business, not of you as a human being. If you come across as someone who can't take constructive criticism, you're going to come across as an amateur or, worse yet, as stubborn and immature. Professionals always treat each meeting as if it were just one of many they're having. Their emotions (even enthusiasm) never overwhelm a meeting. No one ever got financed because the bank felt sorry for him. At least not since most of the S & Ls folded. Instead of worrying about your ego, spend the time worrying about cash. In fact, you'd better get used to spending a lot of time worrying about cash.

All of this risk taking must excite you. You'll need to find a perverse pleasure in lying awake at night wondering how you're going to meet a challenge. Remember: There are problems and there are problems. Some problems are good to have. Deciding whether or not you can afford to run your business anymore is a bad problem. Deciding how you're going to do all the work you've got lined up is a good problem. Lose corresponding amounts of sleep over each one. And even the bad problems are only obstacles. Remember that there are few business problems that can't be solved by human ingenuity and effort. All it takes is confidence.

Karen Bacon was one of the first events planners in New York City. She is a great example of someone who has confidence in herself. "I'm never nervous before a party. I give the impression of total calmness." Making up her job as she went along was challenging, but she always knew she was up to the task. "In my family we always thought that if you knew what you wanted, you could do it. It's almost like a blind spot: People say you can't do it, but you don't hear them and you go ahead and make it work."

Confidence Quiz

- As a student, did you fall asleep easily the night before exams?
  4 *(No)*   3   2   1 *(Yes)*

- As a child, were you successful when you went door to door trick-or-treating or selling candy for school or charities?
  4 *(Unsuccessful)*   3   2   1 *(Successful)*

- How many attempts did it take to pass your driving test?
  4 *(4 or more)*   3   2   1 *(Just one)*

- Assuming you're a capable swimmer and there was no one better qualified around, how willing would you be to risk your life saving someone from drowning?
  4 *(No way)*   3   2   1 *(I'd definitely do it)*

- How much do you enjoy introducing yourself to strangers at parties?
  4 *(Hate it)*   3   2   1 *(Love it)*

Total _____

Even after twenty years, she hasn't allowed herself to get into a rut. "The whole business is a risk, but I did it because it was the kind of work I wanted to do. The risk is always there—you're always on the line, always selling yourself."

Greg Heisler is a free-lance photographer who works for magazines like *Time* and *Life,* as well as doing corporate and advertising work. At a recent workshop he was asked what makes someone a successful photographer. "It's almost as though these people who are successful have always thought of themselves as successful. Even if they're terrible, odd, unpleasant people, they manage to communicate to the person giving the assignment that they can deliver. Two people could be in the room. One could be engaging and pleasant and might actually get a better photograph, but the job would go to the other person because that person somehow knows it's a done deal. Editors like to feel confident about who they are giving an assignment to."

INTEGRITY

In the 21st Century, an entrepreneur will need to have a great deal of integrity. After the excessive eighties, everyone is hyper-aware of anything that doesn't have integrity at its core. We've had enough of frippery and flimflam, and the only way to be truly confident about your service is to have integrity.

Greg Heisler has a reputation as both a great photographer and someone who can be trusted. He says that problems with ethics "come up all the time. The choice is whether to cave in and go for the quick money or stick to your guns morally. Some photographers out there would shoot each other in the foot if they had to. But jobs are hard enough to come by, and clients are even harder to find, so I don't do anything to antagonize the client. If there's a problem, I'm always ready and interested in resolving it in a way to please them and myself." This reputation for straight dealing has served him well. On one occasion, after shooting a picture of George Bush for *Time,* he got a phone call from the magazine's accounting department. There was a question about his bill. "I asked, 'Okay, what is it?' I was all ready for the bad news. And they said, 'We want to pay you more than you charged us because the photo was used as a cover.' "

Integrity Quiz

• What did you do the last time you were given too much change?
  4 *(Pocketed it)*   3   2   1 *(Gave it back)*

• What would you do if you found a wallet, with cash in it, in the street?
  4 *(Pocket the cash)*   3   2   1 *(Hand it in intact)*

• How many times did you cheat on a test in school?
  4 *(At least 4 times)*   3   2   1 *(Once or less)*

• How likely are you to put a "meter broken" sign on a working parking meter?
  4 *(Do it all the time)*   3   2   1 *(People do that?)*

Total _____

COMMON SENSE

Common sense is a classic characteristic of all successful businessmen and women and was as important in colonial America as it will be in the new century. Clearly, if you're going to be handling thousands of dollars of other people's money, you need to be grounded in reality. You need to be able to step outside yourself and observe, with an unbiased eye, what is happening to you and your business.

Elysa Lazar is president of the Lazar Media Group, an organization that puts out, among other things, *The S&B Report,* a newsletter that lists shopping bargains. She has some strong things to say about common sense. "Oh, it's very important. I think people get caught up in what they think they should be doing, rather than doing what they know they ought to be doing. If you're smart, trust your instincts, don't rely on formulas. If you think you're making a mistake, stop. If you think you should take a risk, then take it. Apply the same principles to your business as you would to your personal finances."

Common Sense Quiz

* How easy would it be for you to reconnect all the wires behind your stereo?
  4 *(I couldn't do it)*   3   2   1 *(No sweat)*

* How easy would it be for you to program your VCR?
  4 *(Can't change the clock)*   3   2   1 *(No sweat)*

* Do you do things the way you were taught or the way that makes sense to you?
  4 *(Their way)*   3   2   1 *(I do it my way)*

* Can you light a wood fire?
  4 *(Only with lighter fluid)* 3 2 1 *(With just two sticks)*

Total _____

CREATIVITY

Common sense will get you only so far. Sooner or later you're going to need to come up with some creative solutions. Your two major problems will be limited finances and finding clients. While careful money management will prevent most catastrophes, you'll find that from time to time sudden insights will help you reach

Creativity Quiz

It's hard to test for creativity. We've come up with a few questions, but they'll take more time to answer than the previous ones. What's most important here is to assess your past careers and other parts of your life. Look back at your school career. Did you always come up with oddball ideas, original thoughts? Have you been an innovator and a freethinker? Or have you been a follower? Remember, if you haven't been completely creative, it doesn't mean you won't be a wonderful entrepreneur, it's just going to affect the way you come up with your entrepreneurial idea. A creative person might come up with an original idea; a less creative person should concentrate on adapting someone else's (more on that in Chapter Five). Here are three tasks psychologists have used to measure creativity:

- How many different uses for an old tire can you think of? _____

- How could you adapt a tool or household appliance so that it works better? _____

  _____

  _____

- Draw a circle on each of twenty sheets of paper. Then create twenty different drawings around the circles.

To evaluate how you did, first ask whether you enjoyed taking the test. If you did, then—however good or bad your solutions—you're probably a creative person. You could also ask a friend you consider to be either creative or not at all creative to do the same tasks and see how you compare.

a new level of success. At the most unlikely moment (as you pick your cat up from the vet, for instance) a solution will come to you.

Learn from others. Creativity is expressed in different ways by people all the time. It's up to you to find out how they're doing it. Watch, learn, and be open-minded.

For example, keep an eye on your television. Soon it's going to be replaced by something with infinitely more potential for creativity. You won't just sit and watch it, you'll be involved. Certain people are going to tap into this new medium and create art we can only dream about as yet. One of these people is Gregg Trueman, president of NeoGraphics, a graphic design company that is exploring the possibilities of using graphics and sound with computers. "My interest isn't in settling down and growing a business. I want to ride the wave of technology until the business gets to where I want to go, which will be more towards interactive multimedia."

FLEXIBILITY

Closely allied to creativity, but easier to learn, is flexibility. We've stated that one of a small business's greatest assets is its flexibility. It stands to reason that you, too, must be flexible. Although you must be focused in order to achieve your goal, you also need to be open to trying different means to achieve the same end. Your goal is to be running a successful business. You'll define success with your own mixture of financial and spiritual reward. How you get there depends on your ability to adapt and survive. For example, let's say you plan to repair computers, but during the first few months you realize that most of the computers you fix have broken down because they're too dirty. So you change the direction of the company to one that specializes in preventative maintenance.

Gregg Trueman is determined to stay flexible. He knows the computer-design industry is changing too quickly for a small business to get pegged as doing one thing. "Right now we're digitizing video and editing it on the computer, making computer-generated movies. Somewhere along the way I may stumble on something that may become my life work." Many people are flexible in the way they make enough money to survive: We know one man who is an actor and singer in a band and who actually makes his living by typesetting for various magazines.

Flexibility Quiz

* How many weeks has it been since you tried a new food?
  4 *(Or more)*   3   2   1 *(Or less)*

* Do you always wear the same combinations of clothes?
  4 *(Every day)*   3   2   1 *(Rarely if ever)*

* How many curses would you utter if you had to take a detour on the way home?
  4 *(Or more)*   3   2   1 *(Or none)*

* At the start of a new year, how many weeks does it take you to stop writing the previous year on your checks?
  4 *(Or more)*   3   2   1 *(Or less)*

Total _____

DEDICATION AND MOTIVATION

If you think you're going to do less work when you start your own business, take this book right back to the bookstore. There just aren't enough hours in a day for the successful entrepreneur. In fact, at some point, all new business owners wish there was an extra day in the week. Monday comes around too soon, and there are always things to do. When was the last time you wished for an extra work day at your current job? Just as money takes on an extra "spiritual" value, so time becomes transformed when you're an entrepreneur. When you worked for someone else you were standing on the bank, looking upstream, watching the hours, days and minutes roll past in the water. You marked time in terms of the vacations coming to you, the paychecks due on the first and fifteenth of every month, and, eventually, retirement.

Not so for the 21st Century entrepreneur. By launching your rickety ship on the river and heading upstream, you expose yourself to more risks, but you certainly get to experience more. A magical thing happens. The months and years suddenly become less important. You're aware of time passing, but your attention is on your boat, your company. You become focused on what's important: you, your business, and anyone else you happen to have brought along for the ride. Nothing is going to distract you once you start your business. You won't have time for jobs around the house (for the first few months anyway), and your weekend softball game is going to suffer. But remember, you'll be motivated because you're thrilled and excited, not because you're afraid of getting fired by your unappreciative boss.

Insurance broker Ed Alleva, Jr., of Brooklyn, New York, has this to say about running a service business: "Think of it as boxing. Each day is like being in the ring for two minutes. It's real tough. Some days you take a hit, some days you give a punch. But it's exciting and you always get something out of the day that makes you feel good about yourself and what you're doing." It's not all going to be rewarding and fun. Tedium is going to rear its ugly head from time to time. And not every customer is going to want to tap into your creative depths. You'll need to be able to work carefully through less than stimulating tasks with an eye toward the more interesting projects that will be coming your way. You'll need to have a bright outlook on life to take you through these times.

Photographer Greg Heisler, despite his world-class reputation, still finds that business ebbs and flows. "I always tend to be madly optimistic," he says. "Even now, when it's been a bit of a hard time, I've been optimistic. I feel that if I never worked again in the U.S., I could just go somewhere else. I think dwelling on 'woe is me' doesn't help. People just pick up on my enthusiasm. There's lots of photos out there to be taken!'' Illustrator Anna Walker had to begin her free-lance career by taking her portfolio to different companies. This took a great deal of determination. ''My stuff is different,'' she says. ''I make small three-D models and photograph them. That's good because people like to play with them. Unfortunately, people's reactions have nothing to do with whether they'll hire you. Sometimes the people who like my work the most never call me back; sometimes the people who just grunt end up calling me back.''

Finally, you must be dedicated to perfection. Excellence is one sure way to success in the 21st Century. Value for money is no longer enough: You must give excellent value at an appropriate price. If you provide a superior service, then you'll be positioned to reap the benefits.

Dedication and Motivation Quiz

- When you work somewhere, do you do the bare minimum or do you give your all?
  4 *(The less the better)*   3   2   1 *(Whatever it takes)*

- How many days a week do you take off the entire time you're allowed for lunch?
  4 *(Four or more)*   3   2   1 *(Once at most)*

- Did you try out for teams or clubs or plays at school, even though you weren't certain of getting picked?
  4 *(Never)*   3   2   1 *(All the time)*

- If you enjoy the first part of a TV miniseries, do you watch the rest?
  4 *(Rarely)*   3   2   1 *(Always)*

Total _____

EDUCATION, EXPERIENCE, AND EXPERTISE

One thing many currently successful entrepreneurs have in common is a parent who is or was an entrepreneur. Don't worry if your father was a lifelong paper pusher for IBM. This doesn't mean your company is doomed. However, it does mean you should think about why this father/child connection exists. The most obvious reason is that the children actually experienced the whole process of starting a business. They saw that "it could be done." They saw their parents, with all their flaws, managing to support their families while pursuing their dreams. And most children think, "If they can do it, then so can I, and probably better too." Also, the parents were probably able to provide both wisdom and work experience. Time served in the family firm is usually a famously unpleasant chore, but it also gives the child great experience. And previous experience in the field they've entered is another common factor among successful business people. No matter how little faith sons and daughters have in their parents' wisdom, from time to time they'll pay attention and a nugget will probably seep in. This is certainly what happened to Ed Alleva, Jr. "It took me ten years to learn the business from my father, and it wasn't easy. But I knew I had to learn from him before I could do it my way. He taught me that we were running the business for a reason, that we were here to help people. And that's what I think about every day."

It's currently fashionable to laugh at the idea of earning an M.B.A. Americans cling to the frontier-bred distrust of "book-larnin'." However, for people who lack the hands-on experience of working for a family firm, or for people who want to get a wider knowledge of business rather than relying on Dad's hoary advice, then an M.B.A. is the way to go.

However, even having an M.B.A. from Harvard and having a self-made billionaire as a father is no guarantee of success. Only you hold that guarantee. You can educate yourself, reading books like this one, and you can give yourself experience. There's (al-

Education, Experience, and Expertise Quiz

By now you should know whether or not you have the dedication to gain more expertise, experience, or education. Examine what areas you're already an expert in. Work from your strengths. In Chapters Four through Six we'll help you come up with the idea for your service business. You'll need to ask yourself what you need to learn before you can begin. For now, consider the following situations:

- You've been invited to appear on "The Tonight Show." What subjects would you feel most comfortable having Jay Leno ask you about? _____

  _____

  _____

- You've reached the finals of the Tournament of Champions on "Jeopardy." What four categories are you hoping Alex Trebek will announce are on the board? _____

  _____

  _____

- Your neighbor's son, who has just graduated from Harvard, wants you to explain something to him. What would you choose to explain? _____

  _____

  _____

most) nothing that you can't do. And what you can't do, you can hire someone else to do for you.

TOUGH LOVE

When you discipline your child, even though it upsets him and makes you feel guilty, then you're dealing out "tough love." The ability to use it is a crucial skill possessed by any successful parent, whether of a business or a child. As the 21st Century approaches and businesses develop and grow faster and faster, you'll find yourself having to exercise this skill sooner than someone starting ten or fifteen years ago would have had to. Your grace period will be short, and tough decisions will need to be made all the time. You must be aware of three areas in which you'll need to remain clear-sighted, hard-hearted, and true to your principles.

WITH YOUR FINANCES

You'll love your business and you'll go to any lengths to keep it healthy. That's why you must be careful. You can't afford to go to any lengths to keep it afloat. We'll talk more about this in subsequent chapters, but you need to know when to cut your losses.

WITH YOUR EMPLOYEES

We think that if you're smart, none of your employees will be your children or other members of your family. We believe family members can be partners, but not employees. (We'll get into our reasons for this belief later in Chapter Fourteen, but for now, please just go along with us.) You may not have any employees at all in the beginning, but if you do, treat them as well as you can, perhaps making up in respect what you can't afford to pay in salary or benefits. The key to a successful relationship with your employees is to make your expectations clear from the start. Be aware that they aren't as interested in your business as you are and you can't expect them to give the 150 percent you're giving. In other words, cut them some slack and expect, at best, 100 percent effort.

On the other hand, if they don't do their jobs well—politely, efficiently, and cheerfully—fire them. It's only fair to you, your family, your investors, and to the other employees: Why should someone work hard if others are getting away with being lazy?

WITH YOUR CUSTOMERS

Isn't the customer always right? Doesn't he or she always know best? Well, yes and no. Often clients will come to you with some vague ideas, and it's up to you to lead them through the fog. They'll think they want to go one way, and you'll know they should go the other way. They're paying you for your expertise, and you must live up to their expectations. Just as you need to be honest with your own family and child, even if it hurts, so you must level with the client. Any client who can't accept your honesty, integrity, and tough love probably isn't going to remain your client anyway. When dealing with recalcitrant clients you should be just as gentle as you would be with a child, but even more honest.

Sooner or later you're going to end up with a prize ass for a client. Then you must decide whether the strain he is putting on you and your staff is worth the money you're being paid. If it is, grin, bear it, and double the fee next time. If it's not, resign the account. Don't worry, you won't be the first to let this person go, and your circle of business associates will probably respect you for it.

Most free-lancers have stories about employers who show a complete lack of scruples. "There are lots of ethical problems in advertising," says Greg Heisler. "There's something called a swipe where a client rips out something from a magazine and says, 'Shoot something like this for me,' or sometimes they just say, 'Shoot this.' I refer them back to the person who shot the original picture. One pharmaceutical company essentially copied a famous Pulitzer Prize-winning photographer's picture and wanted me to do it. I told them to go back to the original person.

They said, 'Thank you very much,' and went off and found some-one else to fake it.''

Tough Love Quiz

* How overweight is your pet (assuming you have one)?
  4 *(Very)*   3   2   1 *(Not at all)*

* How long would you be willing to let a spoiled child cry?
  4 *(About ten seconds)*   3   2   1 *(Until he or she stopped)*

* How many dates would you go on with someone before you revealed that you hated his cologne or her perfume?
  4 *(Or more)*   3   2   1 *(Or on the first)*

* How many credit cards do you have in your wallet?
  4 *(Or more)*   3   2   1 *(Or none)*

Total _____

WHAT YOUR SCORE MEANS

Add all your scores together for the sections with numeric an-swers to see which of the following categories you fit into. If you're on the cusp between two categories, try to factor in the results of the sections without numeric scores and adjust your category up or down one notch.

25

You're either lying or you should forget about starting a busi-ness and instead apply to the Vatican for sainthood. The fact is, no entrepreneur is going to be perfect, just as no parent can be. That's why bankruptcy lawyers and therapists exist (two fine ser-vice businesses, we might add!).

26 TO 36

What have you been waiting for? You believe you have what it takes to become a 21st Century entrepreneur. You're well set to succeed.

38 TO 54

You're almost there. You seem to have what it takes. Go back and check the sections on "Dedication and Motivation" and "Confidence." If you had only two 3s or one 4 on those sections, you'll be fine.

55 TO 83

Be careful. You have many of the qualities needed, but go back and examine any of the sections where you chose a 4 and see if you really have what it takes. You may just need to gain more experience.

83 TO 100

Don't quit your day job. You don't seem to have the personality traits and characteristics that most entrepreneurs possess.

Regardless of your particular score, it's essential to look at the areas you need to work on and make a conscious effort to remedy them as you continue to plan your own business. That's a process we begin in the next chapter as we help you decide what type of service business yours should be.

For more information on the topics covered in Chapter 3, take a look at the following book:

- *Have You Got What It Takes: How to Tell If You Should Start Your Own Business,* by Joseph R. Mancuso (Prentice-Hall, 1982)

4

CANNONBALL CREATIVITY

Jumping into the 21st Century

You can't come up with an idea for a 21st Century business unless you're immersed in the 21st Century. You need to be able to step out of your everyday mind set and visualize where America and the world will be in the year 2000. Not an easy thing to do when you're living in the 1990s. We suggest that, until Sony comes up with a time machine (probably portable, about the size of a wristwatch), the best way for you to enter the future is to practice what we call *cannonball creativity*. Remember when you were ten years old at the swimming pool? The fastest and easiest way to get into the water was to run at the pool, jump, pull your legs up, and become a human cannonball. It was ungainly but very effective. You're going to jump like this into the waters of the 21st Century.

This is a process that will take a couple of weeks at least. Arrange your life so you can concentrate. Take some time off work if possible, but don't think of it as a vacation—you're going to work intensively. Finding the right idea for your business is a matter of starting with general concepts that can be gradually narrowed down, rather than choosing one idea and sticking with it blindly. Appendix A sums up the whole process in a chart form.

Your first goal: to put aside your personal thoughts and soak up what's important to society. A couple of words of warning. First, don't let what society says is important sway you. Everyone agrees education is important, but we don't pay teachers as though they were professionals. Everyone agrees too much television is bad for children, yet we let our kids watch two hundred thousand commercials before they reach first grade. You're looking for what's really important to society, not what it thinks or says is important. Second: You're looking for long-lasting trends. Take care you don't latch on to a mere fad—a pet rock doth not a trend make. Had the pet rock been followed by the pet vegetable, the pet sofa, and the pet soft drink, then it would have been a trend.

You'll need to devise your own technique of cannon-balling—just as you did when you were ten years old—but what follows should give you some ideas.

WATCH TELEVISION SHOWS YOU DON'T NORMALLY WATCH

If you don't have cable, spend a weekend with someone who does. Make sure you have a notebook and a copy of *TV Guide*. You won't be great company, but by Monday morning you'll know a lot about the workings of the American mind. Pay careful attention to the details in the staging and casting of the shows, as well as the ads. New season pilots are particularly interesting. See if you can predict which shows will be continued and which will be canceled, and why. It's a trend-watching truism that if an idea has reached television, it's firmly fixed in the national psyche.

READ PUBLICATIONS YOU DON'T NORMALLY READ

Go to the largest news agent in town and spend fifty dollars on specialized magazines. Read magazines aimed at ethnic groups different from your own. Or, if you're a man, read *Family Circle;* if you're a woman, read *Soldier of Fortune.* Buy *Bow Hunter: The Magazine for the Hunting Archer*—don't laugh, it has a circulation of 250,000. Buy *Working Mother Magazine*—it has a circulation of 700,000. Buy magazines from other cities or regions. If you live in the Northeast, buy *Los Angeles.* If you live in the southeast, buy *Snow Country.* Read the small ads—even the classified ads—to see who the advertisers think the readers are. Make notes and see if you can find common threads and patterns.

DRIVE DOWNTOWN, TO ANOTHER TOWN, OR TO THE MALL

Once you arrive at your location, buy a newspaper and sit on a bench observing people at lunch and at play. Get a haircut and ask the barber or stylist what's on his or her mind. Get in a taxicab and ask impertinent questions. Eavesdrop on everyone and apologize to no one—you're on a mission: to boldly go where no man or woman has gone before . . . the 21st Century! Sure, you'll become an inquisitive pest; but don't worry about what other people think. The 21st Century entrepreneur knows information is power and that for the first time since before the Industrial Revolution, people are giving away power for free.

Power during the Industrial Revolution was created by expensive machines like the cotton gin and the sewing machine. In those days you needed a great deal of money to buy the necessary machines. In effect, you needed money to make money. In the 21st Century most everyone can readily afford the necessary machines—computers, telephones, and faxes. It's having information that will enable you to make money. Because of this, you, as a flexible, responsive individual, have the advantage over lumbering corporations. A large corporation has to commission a survey firm and spend months and millions to find out what people think. All you need do is ask your neighbors.

ANALYZE YOUR OWN LIFE

What would you have someone else do for you if the price was right? We've decided it's worth the cost to pay someone to come in and clean our apartment every week. However, we think it's not worth it to pay someone to come in and organize our closets. We'll get around to that next month . . . perhaps.

LISTEN TO THE TREND TRACKERS

BrainReserve, one of America's top trend-spotting companies, was founded by Faith Popcorn almost twenty years ago. Though

Popcorn is well-known for her unusual name and the catchy moni-
kers she attaches to the trends she spots, she has also shown an
uncanny ability to predict the future. That's why some of America's most successful businesses—from Eastman Kodak to Coca-
Cola—have enlisted her help. That's also why we think you
should pay attention to what she thinks. In her book *The Popcorn
Report,* she describes the following ten trends she believes are
shaping the way we live our lives now and will continue to do
so into the 21st Century:

CASHING OUT

Working women and men will question personal/career satisfaction and goals, and opt for simpler living.

COCOONING

The need to protect oneself from the harsh, unpredictable reali-
ties of the outside world, which Popcorn isolated early in her
trend-tracking career, will become more powerful, perhaps even
turning into Burrowing.

DOWN-AGING

Nostalgic for their carefree childhood, baby boomers will find
comfort in familiar pursuits and the products of their youth.

EGONOMICS

The sterile computer era will breed the desire to make a personal statement.

FANTASY ADVENTURE

The modern age will whet our desire for roads not taken.

NINETY-NINE LIVES

Too fast a pace and too little time will cause societal schizo-
phrenia and force us to assume multiple roles and adapt easily.

SOS (SAVE OUR SOCIETY)

The country will rediscover a social conscience of ethics, passion, and compassion.

SMALL INDULGENCES

Stressed-out consumers will indulge in affordable luxuries and seek ways to reward themselves.

STAYING ALIVE

The awareness that good health extends longevity will lead to a new way of life.

THE VIGILANTE CONSUMER

The consumer will manipulate marketers and the marketplace through pressure, protest, and politics.

Bear in mind that more than one trend can influence a consumer: Our hiring a firm that only uses biodegradable products to clean our apartment involved Popcorn's "Ninety-nine lives," "SOS," and "Small indulgences." The key for you is to observe that the trend is happening, or going to be happening, and then to identify the needs it will create.

While we don't have Faith Popcorn's track record, we have been diving into the 21st Century for quite some time as we researched this book. Here are some fields we think will prove fruitful for entrepreneurs in the 21st Century. After each field, we've given an example of a potential entrepreneurial opportunity:

ECOLOGY

Dealing with the nitty-gritty of recycling is becoming increasingly annoying for consumers.

CHILD CARE

Schools are feeling the need to provide services once provided by the family.

INFORMATION

Consumers will need help to cut through the clutter to find exactly what information they need.

EDUCATION

Is the traditional public school slowly dying? What are the (affordable) alternatives?

RECREATION

Can you teach people to relax without scaring them away with New Age mumbo jumbo?

FOOD

People want to buy organic food, but they think it looks dirty.

HEALTH CARE

It costs too much to get sick. Some savvy entrepreneurs will explore the potential of preventative medicine and save everyone money.

ETHNIC NEEDS

Whatever you think of multiculturalism, it's clearly leading all ethnic groups to feel increasingly comfortable displaying their group's differences and achievements.

SHORTCUTS

Anything and everything will be delivered to your home.

DIGITAL ENTERTAINMENT

Recordable compact disks are already here. Affordable do-it-yourself animation and even home-based virtual reality aren't far behind.

The preceding are examples of fields we think will grow rapidly. But don't forget that there are many other areas of 20th Century life that are going to need to adapt to the 21st Century whether they like it or not. Here are just six examples: the prison system, housing, transportation, infrastructure in cities, and the banking and insurance industries.

Recently in New York City, fifty friends and members of Grace Church School, Greenwich Village's leading private school, sat down together and worked out a long-range plan for the school. People were there from every power center in New York City: political, professional, and social. Here are some of the issues *they* thought needed attention if the students were to succeed in the 21st Century. This is another list that could provide you with some useful starting points in developing ideas.

Practical "hands-on" experience in science, technology, and math

Proficiency in a foreign language upon graduation

Familiarity with other cultures and religions

After a couple of weeks of talking, reading, and viewing, sit back and relax. Sleep. Take a weekend off. Think of yourself as coming out of that pool of information. You've exercised hard and now you're going to relax in the sun.

While you're sunning yourself, let's take a small break to talk about what you've been doing. Psychologists have discovered that when we learn something new, we attach the new fact or thought to already existing "schemata." These schemata are large webs of information we already know. For example, when we learned that people were using fax machines, we attached that fact to everything else we knew about telephones.

The metaphor of the web is an important one for the 21st Century. It conjures up a picture of the fragmented, information-based society that will develop. No longer will we live in the world of the pyramid corporation; instead, customers, small companies, and entrepreneurs will relate to one another in a mutually supporting network of needs and services. (We'll get back to this concept a little later.)

What you've been doing by reading and watching and listening to modern America is creating an invaluable data base of information inside your brain. You could pay a research consultant ten thousand dollars and he wouldn't be able to come up with anything as pertinent to you and your needs. By taking a weekend off, you're allowing your brain to organize the webs into schemata that make sense: It's not filing the information alphabetically, it's making links in the web.

After you've finished relaxing, sit down with a pencil and a large sheet of paper. Write down everything that interests and excites you. Depending on how wide-ranging your interests are, this may take an evening or two. Don't make a list, and don't try to organize the information—just spread the thoughts out all over the page. Be wild! Be crazy! You can always cross off an idea later, but don't stifle yourself. Five years ago, who thought adults would pay vast sums of money to talk dirty to one another? But it's estimated that "adult" 1-900 numbers made $515 million in 1991. Don't worry whether or not the areas are feasible as businesses. If you're interested in unmanned space flight, then write it down. You saw an interesting program about Argentine bats? Write it down. Don't let any preconceived ideas get in the way of your thought processes here.

Next, group together similar subjects and thoughts on another sheet of paper. You'll be surprised at how many links there are.

You may even find that a single concept—for instance, something like ''ecology''—runs through all the subjects. Each of these clusters of thoughts is a field that you're interested in. With luck, you'll have four or five different fields to look at. Some will seem impractical, others merely mundane, but they're all from you, and that means they contain the primary seed of success: your enthusiasm.

For example, the conversation you overheard about your friend Frank wanting to move to Maine is linked to your observation that all sorts of people in the city seem to have cars with four-wheel drive. This doesn't mean that anyone, including Frank, will ever visit Maine or anywhere more demanding than the New Jersey Turnpike, but the cars and the talk of Maine both represent a desire to be able to escape. And that desire is a field for you to examine and perhaps eventually profit from.

The final part of cannonball creativity involves applying a series of common-sense questions to your categories or potential areas of business. By considering the following questions in relation to each field, you'll be able to assess its viability and your own enthusiasm for it. Just like the lifeguard at the pool, you need to make a judgment call and decide whether your dive was done sensibly. With luck, you'll get added points for style.

IS THIS THE SAME FIELD I'M IN NOW?

Clearly you could develop your ideas about your current field if you're working for a résumé-writing service, but it's going to be harder if you're employed by AT&T.

HOW IS NEW TECHNOLOGY GOING TO AFFECT THIS FIELD?

This is a crucial question. In major cities, the blast of bike messengers' whistles and the swoosh as they raced past you was one of the defining experiences of the early and mid-eighties, but the whistles have all but disappeared since the arrival of affordable fax machines. Business people all over the city asked themselves why they should entrust their precious documents to a maniac on a ten-speed when they could send a copy over the phone. The fax was quieter, safer, and cheaper.

But new technology isn't always bad news for a service business associated with the old technology. We know of an old shop that has been repairing typewriters for twenty-four years. It's stayed in business despite the increasing popularity of computers, because of the quality and personal touch of its service, and its location. "There's always going to be typewriters," says the owner. "Who can be bothered to learn a computer if all you've got to do is write a letter? And even computerized offices still use typewriters to address envelopes and write labels. Besides, this is an older community—there are a lot of people here who like typewriters better."

DO I HAVE EXPERIENCE IN THIS FIELD?

Experts estimate that 95 percent of successful new businesses are begun by people who had previous experience in the field. You'll be able to sell your service only if you're an expert. The field may be completely outside your experience, and so you may need to delay starting the business while you gain knowledge. Having said that, it's up to you to define what "experience" and "expert" mean, especially if the field is a new one.

HOW MUCH DOES THIS FIELD EXCITE ME?

This is closely related to the preceding question. Can you remain excited while you learn? Your excitement for the field may need to carry you through a great deal of hard work and worry before you see any money. Ask yourself, "Am I doing this just to make money or am I genuinely excited by it?" A desire to be rich isn't a good enough reason, though it's obviously important. You're going to be working long hours, giving yourself and your friends and family a lot of stress. But take heart: The National Federation of Independent Business found that 83 percent of business owners they surveyed would continue to do what they were doing even if they had enough money to never work again.

HOW CAN I MAKE MONEY DOING THIS?

You can make money from the strangest things. You probably can't make money directly from unmanned space flights or Argentine bats. But there may be people out there who want to know more about space flights or bats. Will they pay for information? You must always remember that in order for your business to succeed, people must be willing to pay to have that need satisfied.

HOW COME NO ONE ELSE IS DOING THIS?

You must decide whether you're the only person looking at this field because you're a crackpot or because you've seen an opportunity no one else has! We'll show you how to evaluate your specific idea later on.

IS THERE A REAL NEED FOR THIS SERVICE?

Be honest with yourself. It's better to admit defeat now than after you've sunk your life savings into the business. Would you pay someone to do this service for you? Are you offering more than sincerity? Of course you believe in your business, but is that earnestness all you're offering?

Having asked yourself all these questions about the various fields you picked, list them in two ways. On one list, rank the fields first in terms of what you want to do most. Then rank them in terms of what you can do best. With luck, the lists will overlap.

Sleep on it, think about it some more. For now, choose the top two or three fields in each list.

FOLLOWING OUR OWN ADVICE

To better illustrate the process of starting a business, we're going to use our own experiences starting a newsletter as a recurring example throughout the rest of the book. The story of our newsletter is fictional, but the important elements—those that illustrate the principles and practices involved in starting a business—are completely accurate.

We took two weeks' vacation from our jobs and set about discovering what service business we wanted to start. We watched daytime television; we watched late night television. We spent three days in the city's central library reading best-sellers and obscure magazines. We packed an overnight bag and headed off into the countryside, leaving our two pet iguanas with our neighbor. Once we got out of the city, we sat in diners and chain restaurants, listening and talking to people, asking them about their hobbies, interests, concerns, and what they wanted to change about their lives. It felt a little like we were running for office.

Finally, when we felt we couldn't eat out another night, we headed back to our home and our iguanas, Iggy and Squiggy. We examined our own lives. We wandered through our apartment picking up books, magazines, pets, and objects, wondering how we could make money from them. We looked at the trends that were going to be important and thought about which of those excited us. Exhausted after ten days of researching and connecting ideas, we sank into a deep sleep, dreaming of trends and consumers and endless line graphs that ran off into the future. The next day, searching for something to do that couldn't be thought of as research, we took Iggy and Squiggy for a walk in the park.

That evening, sitting in front of the fire with a large sheet of blank paper, we started to write down everything that excited us. We filled up two sheets of paper with crazy ideas: everything from repairing lamps, breeding iguanas, writing letters for other people, and becoming fast-food tasters, all the way to repairing gym equipment and organizing people's bookshelves. Then, following our own advice, we got yet another sheet of paper and grouped together any similar ideas. We were surprised to see that most of them fell into six fields: writing, caring for our pets, fixing up antiques, teaching, how information is managed, and eating.

We looked at each group of ideas and asked basic questions: Is this field related to the jobs we're in now? How is new technology going to affect this field? Did we have any experience? Did it excite us? How could we make money from it? Was there a real need for it? We were able to eliminate two fields by answering these questions: We like to fix up old furniture, but we knew we could never get completely enthusiastic about it. We know we enjoy eating, but we doubted whether we would ever get anyone to pay us to do it. Finally we made our two lists, ranking the fields according to those we wanted to do most and those we thought we could do best. As you'll see, the lists did overlap, and so we began to narrow down our choices. In Chapter Five we'll show *you* how to do that.

For more information on the topics covered in Chapter Four, take a look at the following books:

- *Small Business in America: The Year 2000 & Beyond,* by the Naisbett Group (NFIB Foundation, 1986)
- *Toward the Twenty-First Century: The Challenges for Small Business,* edited by Martyn Robertson, Elizabeth Chell, and Colin Mason (Taylor & Francis, 1992)

❊ 5 ❊

PLAY TO WIN

Pinning Down Your Ideas

Now that you've a list of general fields that both interest you and hold out the potential for entrepreneurial success, it's time to refine them and develop some specific ideas for businesses. This process can actually be a lot of fun.

You may be tempted to abandon all but your favorite general idea at this point, but we urge you not to. Confidence is an important entrepreneurial trait, but tunnel vision is a liability. By exploring multiple fields, you not only leave all your options open, but you also allow for cross-pollination to take place. And as we'll see later in this chapter, such combining of concepts from different areas is an excellent way to refine your ideas. With that warning in mind, begin doing some hands-on research into each of your general fields.

RESEARCHING YOUR GENERAL FIELDS

Here are several ways of collecting raw information about each general field.

ASK POTENTIAL CLIENTS AND POTENTIAL RIVALS WHAT THEY WANT, AND THEN ASK THEM WHY THEY WANT IT

It sounds ridiculously obvious, but it's very effective. Adapt this list of simple questions for your own use, then ask them of other people.

1. What annoys you most about (insert your field here)?
2. Why does it annoy you?
3. What do you think was the last significant thing to happen in that field?
4. Why do you think it so significant?
5. Do you feel you're being overcharged for this service?
6. If so, why?
7. If you were running this kind of service, would you make any changes?
8. If so, why?

If someone gives you a good idea, pump him for more information, then ask the next person what he thinks of it.

Here's an example of these questions being used. One of Frank's fields is newspapers. He's trying to find out what his neighbor Albert dislikes about reading the newspaper.

"So, Albert, what annoys you about reading the newspaper?"

"Nothing annoys me about it, Frank. I enjoy it."

"There must be something that annoys you about it."

"Well, I get annoyed when it arrives late."

"Why's that, Albert?"

"You know why, Frank. It means I don't get to read it over breakfast."

"What was the last thing anyone did to make your newspaper delivery better?"

"I guess it was when they started putting old bread bags around the paper on rainy days."

"Are you being overcharged for your newspaper delivery?"

"Well, yes, I am."

"Why's that?"

"Because the darn thing never arrives in time."

"So what would you do to change this?"

"I'd either get rid of that paperboy or buy him a decent bike."

You'll need to use your intelligence to decipher the answers you get. People don't like to be rude about other people or even other businesses. We all try to be polite in conversation, especially with strangers.

Let's imagine that someone is interested in starting an advertising agency and has gathered responses to his version of the second question, "Why does your current advertising agency annoy you?" As you'll see, what people say isn't always what they mean. An experienced market researcher has provided us with a translation.

"They have a lot of big clients and they're well-known in the field. They're always busy." (Translation: "I'm just a small business and I feel neglected by them.")

"I feel like they're experts and they really know what they're doing." (Translation: "I've got no idea how they do what they do.")

"I don't like the way they send a bill every month." (Translation: "Beyond specific projects, the only communication I get from them is the regular bill.")

"They seem to charge the going rate." (Translation: "Someone else must be cheaper. Maybe I'll shop around.")

"They charge too much." (Translation: "I choose to stay with them for some reason: They are prestigious, give impeccable service, etc.")

Make sure you cover all the possible sources. Talk to people outside your immediate group of friends. Pretend you're a freelance journalist if you must. You can set yourself up as a "consultant" for a month or two while you conduct your research. Go into bars and coffee shops. Go to company picnics. Accept that Tupperware party invitation, especially if you're a man. Just be plain nosy. You'll be surprised how many people will pour out their ideas to you. Ask questions of the people you play softball with. Ask your mother and her kaffeeklatsch; they'll love you and put you in touch with all their children. Ask bartenders. They're the village gossips of the late twentieth century, and if they don't know or don't care, they'll point out someone else in the bar who can help you.

Talking to people in the business is obviously a smart thing to do. They won't know, or won't care, that you're a potential rival: They have a false sense of security—they think they're way ahead of you. The truth is, you're climbing on their shoulders, ready to leapfrog over them as soon as you have your financing in place. Trade fairs are useful places to find out about the strengths and weaknesses of a general field. They're also gold mines of gossip. Sit yourself down in the coffee shop at the convention center and strike up conversations with your future rivals. Whenever you talk to someone in the business, act as enthusiastically naive as possible, by asking completely open-ended questions. You don't want "yes" or "no," you want "Well, in my experience, that sort of thing only works when . . ." Don't worry. Everyone thinks he or she is an expert and will be pleased as punch that at long last, someone has asked for advice.

READ MAGAZINES ABOUT YOUR BUSINESS

Go back to the news agent where you bought *Bow Hunter* and *Working Mother*. Buy every magazine relevant to each of your fields. Look at the ads in the back for other magazines aimed at the same consumer and order sample copies. Make notes about who advertises in all of them.

GO TO THE PUBLIC LIBRARY OR THE NEAREST COLLEGE LIBRARY

In any well-stocked library, you'll find copies of *The Encyclopedia of Associations, The Oxbridge Directory of Newsletters,* and *The Encyclopedia of Business Information Services.* Look up "service industries" and you'll see a large number of associations and newsletters, some of which may be useful. Look up your fields and the chances are that someone will be writing a newsletter about it. Most people are happy to send you a sample copy before you commit your money. Contact business associations that are in fields related to the ones you're interested in. They often have conventions and conferences that will be useful for you, as well as newsletters and general guidelines about the business.

If you're lucky enough to have access to a business school library, find the call number of a book that interests you, then wander through the stacks near it. Serendipity is the mother of discovery! Keep an eye out for publications from the U.S. Department of Commerce: Surprisingly, its information is often tailored to local markets.

If your library has the facilities, try searching for magazine articles through a computerized data base like Nexis or Dialog. You feed in a couple of words (''health care'' and ''children,'' for example), and the computer searches for all recent magazine articles on that subject. It can be expensive to obtain full text copies of the articles you uncover, but many libraries will do a bibliographic search for you free, print out a list for you, and send you off to the periodical room to find the articles.

CONTACT THE U.S. SMALL BUSINESS ADMINISTRATION

The SBA puts out a number of useful books and pamphlets. They also have a network of locally run offices. Contact the District Offices, Small Business Development Centers, the local Service Corps of Retired Executives, and nearby Small Business Institutes, and request information on your field. The SBA may be able to help you get in touch with State Economic Development Agencies and local chambers of commerce, which may also be of some assistance.

TAP INTO A COMPUTER BULLETIN BOARD LIKE COMPUSERVE OR PRODIGY

Discuss your ideas with people over the computer, if you're comfortable using a modem. Compuserve is better for people with more computer experience; Prodigy is better for those with less. We have found people are far more likely to be honest when they know they won't be identified. They don't see the anonymity as an opportunity to be mischievous.

Look over all the information you've gathered. Think about it. Look for connections and patterns. Imagine you're a kid again. You've taken out the box of building blocks and you're just about to start playing. You can make anything your imagination will let you. Give yourself a couple of days to let the information sink in. What you're doing is processing raw information and turning it into intelligence, which can then be used to further your goal of starting a service business. The next step is to figure out exactly what that business will be.

There are really only two methods for coming up with a business idea. You either develop an original concept, or steal one that's been proven to work. Of the two, stealing is obviously easier, and it's just as satisfying.

THE COPYCAT METHOD

The copycat method consists of finding someone who is already doing something successfully and adapting the idea. You can do it better and charge your customer more because of all the research you did. You've studied trends and analyzed how technology is going to help or hinder the service. Instead of adapting your business's structure and emphasis to keep pace with new technology, you can jump right in, learning from the competition's mistakes and building on their strengths.

Another great thing about a copycat business is that potential investors and your customers can compare it to something that already exists. They can be convinced what you're going to do is better. As we'll discover in the chapter on financing, convincing people there's a need for a service that doesn't exist can be quite a challenge.

Not only is it easier to get financing for a copycat business, but because you provide better service, you can charge more. One of the most extraordinary things about service businesses is the pricing of the service. We'll talk about this in detail later on, but it's a fact that people believe they get what they pay for, so you're apt to do better if you charge more.

Whatever you do, please don't have any qualms about basing your business on someone else's idea. The day that ideas become the sole property of individuals is the day the American republic should shut up shop and retire. America was founded on ideas Thomas Paine and Jefferson "stole" from French and English philosophers. IBM used to make mechanical adding machines—it didn't come up with the idea of computers.

The idea you copy doesn't need to be from the same field. It's easy to see how to take products from one area and adapt them to a new one (dot matrix printers were originally attached to gambling machines in Las Vegas!), but the same can be done with services. Advertising and real estate agencies first came up with the idea of small, glossy promotional brochures that described their businesses. These brochures were sent out to clients and potential clients and were displayed in the offices. Nowadays, you'll see the same kind of brochure in law firms and accountants' offices. If it's a good idea and it works, then steal it.

DEVELOPING AN ORIGINAL CONCEPT

Much has been written about creativity, but no one has been able to provide a surefire formula for it. We haven't discovered it either, but we have thought long and hard about how new ideas are developed, and have come up with one suggestion: synthesize. Take all the general fields on your lists and write them on individual index cards. Spread the cards out on a table facedown. Turn two over. Then think of a business combining both fields. It doesn't matter if it seems outrageous or fanciful, just keep at it. Once you've done it with combinations of two fields, try it with three.

The idea behind this is simple: You've already determined these fields are interesting to you as well as potentially important to society in the 21st Century. Big businesses and most other entrepreneurs will be thinking about the individual fields and developing the obvious ideas. You, however, will be looking at where these fields intersect and developing the less obvious ideas. Sure, we may not be talking about huge markets—at least not at first. But a small service business doesn't need a huge market to succeed. All it needs is a market whose needs aren't being currently met. We'll talk more about markets in Chapter Six, but for now, suffice it to say that smaller is better.

Here are a couple of examples of synthesized creativity. We sat down and wondered, for example, what happens when you put "education" with "international expansion"? We know that for the first time ever, the ability to speak a foreign language will be an essential part of a child's education, not just a luxury. If the public school system doesn't teach languages well enough to children, then there will be an opportunity for entrepreneurs to open language schools, or offer child-level cassette courses, to pick up the slack. Then we sat down and mixed "health care" with "ecology." We noted that large hospitals are ecologically (and often economically) unsound. Perhaps there will be a return to small "cottage" hospitals offering personal service and value for money, while being more aware of the environment.

Don't let your development of copycat or original ideas be inhibited by questioning whether or not the ideas will work. After all, children at play know that using their imaginations, they can make anything from a space station to the aliens that attack it. Feasibility is something you'll begin checking in Chapter Six. Right now what we're going to do is pin down who or what your customer is going to be.

The world is filled with literally millions of different customer markets. Picking which one you'll be addressing is really an individualized process, based on your specific idea. However, all entrepreneurs must begin by deciding whether they're going to be selling their services to businesses or to individuals.

SELLING YOUR SERVICE TO INDIVIDUALS

You'll find that selling to individuals has certain advantages over selling to businesses, the most important of which is that you are an individual. You can think like your customers, you can put yourself in their shoes, you can experience their feelings. Everyone is a consumer. Some are happier about it than others, but the fact is, everyone consumes. Compare a punk rocker with the phrase "Born, Buy, Consume, Die" scrawled on the back of his leather jacket to a woman wearing a T-shirt with the motto "Born to shop!" silk-screened across the chest. They have different attitudes toward the consumer culture, but both acknowledge that (for better or worse) acquiring and preparing to acquire is how the human race spends a large part of its time.

One disadvantage to dealing with individuals rather than businesses is that if yours is an original service, you'll need to educate individuals before you can sell anything to them. You'll need to explain to each person that it makes sense for him or her to pay you money to do whatever it is. Another problem is that people are capricious. When they see something different, they may forsake your service and try out the new one for the sake of novelty. This is why the quality and value that you offer will be crucial. You'll need to create a solid, loyal base of customers who'll recommend you to their friends—you can't expect to perpetually discover new customers.

This capriciousness isn't all bad news, however. After all, it may be what initially attracts consumers to your service. And in some businesses, attrition is essential. Exercise studios would burst at the seams if they kept all their customers. They count on a steady rate of attrition to make room for new members. We know a gym that occasionally raises its membership fees just to thin the place out. But it's safe to say that, as a general rule, you want to develop loyalty from your customers. (We'll discuss how that's done in Chapter Thirteen.)

There are two ways of servicing individuals: face-to-face, like a car mechanic and a dentist, or through an interface of some sort. Currently that interface is a combination of mail and telephone. The explosion of mail-order catalogs at the end of the eighties was a great example of how popular this method of servicing individuals has become. To most people, J. Crew consists of a catalog full of practical clothes worn by good-looking models doing the relaxing things we can only wish we had time for. The only human contact is with the softly accented "order consultants" on the other end of the phone. By offering an attractive interface consisting of a disembodied voice and a classy catalog, J. Crew has created an entire company image.

Increasingly, by using a fax or a touch-tone phone, the interface will dispense with the voice altogether, returning once more to the anonymity of the mail system. Today you can order food from restaurants, make musical requests of radio stations, and purchase an incredible variety of products via the fax machine. Using a touch-tone phone, you can tune in to pay-per-view TV and choose what movie you want to see or even what music video you want on next. You can even call government offices and be confused by a touch-tone system rather than by real live humans.

If you intend to run a strictly "face-to-face" service business, you'll find that you yourself must become the attractive wrapping around your service. You'll need to have, or develop, a certain attitude. We have a friend who was a terrible waiter because he was doing the job purely for the money . . . and his face showed it. His attitude led to minimal tips, which led to his attitude becoming even more unpleasant, leading to even lower tips. We advised him to quit waiting on tables and to take a job with a telephone sales company. Initially he was no keener to ask strangers questions on the phone than he had been to wait on tables. But because he was insulated from his customers by the interface, he managed to remain charming. He's turned into a successful telephone salesman.

SELLING YOUR SERVICE TO BUSINESSES

In many ways businesses will become the market of preference for the 21st Century entrepreneur. Some experts believe that 95 percent of all jobs will be in service industries by the year 2000. Clearly those businesses will need servicing themselves. One wonderful thing about dealing with other businesses is that most of the time they'll be using other people's money. It's a lot easier to convince someone to spend fifty dollars an hour of his company's money than fifty dollars of his own. You can't charge a business as much as an individual, but companies will give you a larger volume of regular business. And consistent business will pay off in the end.

Another clear advantage of servicing businesses is that, unlike the man in the street, they aren't capricious. Once businesses have a policy and a service to execute the policy, they tend to stick with it. It's easier for them to stay with something that works rather than switch for the sake of trying something new. It's also simpler to see what exactly a business needs in the way of services. And if one business needs something, then chances are, all of its competitors will need it too. You need to be careful, of course: A manager can hide behind other people's decisions if he has to tell you no, you're too expensive. An individual might find it harder to reject you.

The recent and ongoing trend toward corporate streamlining and downsizing will actually help you when dealing with businesses. You'll find that access to the people in charge is easier now. Upper management is less complacent. No one wants to be the person who has to say, "Oh, I didn't think of trying that" to the CEO. Also, every layoff is a potential job for you. Frequently the work still needs to be done, but the company doesn't want to deal with more full-time employees than it absolutely must. When a company deals with consultants and free-lancers, it doesn't need to pay their contributions to Social Security. It also rids itself of all those expensive benefits, particularly health insurance. All that results in a savings of about 20 percent (and climbing) over the cost of a full-time employee. Although you might feel like a vulture circling its prey, the period right after a series of layoffs at a company is a great time to pick up new business.

Once you've thought about the relative advantages of selling to individuals and businesses, you are almost ready to decide on your actual idea. At the end of Chapter 4 you had arranged your ideas for businesses into a number of fields that you thought looked promising. You ranked these fields in two lists—one according to your interest, the other according to your ability. By now you have looked into each general field in a little more depth. You've tried to come up with a specific idea for a business, either original or adopted from someone else's, and you've thought about selling your service to individuals or businesses.

During this process specific ideas for a business will have been popping into your mind. You will have been refining them as you find more information. Now is the time to stop being open-minded and to allow yourself to consider the ideas that are your favorites.

Write them all down, pick the top two or three, and sleep on them. It'll quickly become clear which one your heart is in. And just because you must put some ideas aside doesn't mean that they're lost forever. Take a ten-minute break and congratulate yourself. All that research has paid off: You've an idea for a service business in a field that's going to take off into the 21st Century.

STILL FOLLOWING OUR OWN ADVICE

At the end of Chapter Four we described how we had decided on the fields we were interested in: writing, caring for our pets, teaching, and managing information. We had quickly eliminated fixing up old furniture and eating as business prospects. Looking back on it now, the direction in which we were heading seems obvious, but it took answering the questions and following the procedures from this chapter to really refine our idea.

We pestered everyone we knew, and many, many people we'd never met before. We asked them the set questions: What annoys you most about . . . ? What has changed? Are you overcharged? What would you change? And Why? Why? Why? Why?

We examined each field separately, then in conjunction with another field. The first field we looked at was writing. Both of us enjoyed writing and had written for magazines, so it was natural for us to consider setting ourselves up as free-lance writers. Obviously we would be selling our services to businesses. We asked some friends in the publishing business about the prospects of careers in this field. They were unanimously pessimistic about it. They said that writing a book was about the hardest way to earn a pittance they'd ever come across. They also said that you have to write the book before it's accepted. We knew from our experience that writing articles for magazines can be fun, but that the income is never steady.

Someone suggested writing copy for catalogs or company reports. Apparently the work pays quite well because it's so tedious. But we didn't want to put our personal finances on the line for something so unrewarding. We didn't reject writing completely, though; we felt that our final choice still might have something to do with writing.

Teaching was something else we both enjoyed. We were impatient, though. In order to be working for ourselves, we would have to start up a tutoring business, because neither of us was qualified enough to start up a school. Talking to the owner of a tutoring company in a nearby town confirmed our suspicions: Tutoring was a hard business to expand. To begin with, the hours of the day during which children can be tutored are limited. We also realized that if we hired more tutors to work for us, then we'd spend our time monitoring the tutors rather than teaching. We did like the idea of passing on information to other people, though. We felt that was something we were good at.

This last thought tied in with the third field we had examined—managing information. The amount of available information on any given subject has increased enormously over the last fifty years. We knew from our own experience, though, that too much information can be as bad as too little. (We have seventy channels on our television set, and yet, unless we sit down with the TV listings and plan what we're going to see, we tend to channel-surf for a few minutes and then switch off.) We knew that solving the problem of too much information was going to be an incredible growth area for the 21st Century entrepreneur, but we couldn't quite see how we could be part of the solution.

That left our interest in pets. Iggy and Squiggy were like children to us; ugly children who ate insects, to be sure, but we found we cared enormously about the two of them. Other pet owners we talked to felt similarly about their pets. Deep down we suspected everyone believed that the health and intelligence of their pets reflected something about them. People also felt they had to know something about their pets, something more than just what to feed them and how much exercise they should get. Just as they felt a duty to their children to make sure that they had the best of everything possible, they felt their pets should have as many advantages as possible. This feeling intrigued us, despite its absurdity. We were well aware that Iggy and Squiggy probably just looked upon us as large, unappetizing insects, yet we felt morally obliged to go down to the pet store and get the type of flies we were told are best for iguanas. And all this devotion was to please an impassive, unresponsive beast like the iguana. How, we wondered, must people feel if they owned affectionate, responsive animals like dogs?

We decided to explore this further. We went to the pet store and the library and looked up titles of books and magazines on pets. Of course, there were books devoted to the raising of all sorts of different animals. However, we didn't want to write a book; we wanted a project that could carry on over a number of years. There were whole magazines devoted to particular types of pets and their care. *Mushing* is a magazine that covers "all aspects of sled dog sport." *Pet Health News* covers health care for all animals, from birds to horses. We discovered magazines like *American Pigeon Journal* and *Better Beagling.* There were also lots of newsletters as well: *National Ferret Fancier, The Pomeranian Review,* and two about aardvarks—*Aardvarks in the News* was our favorite title. The incredible number of such specialized publications proved to us that each pet is a market niche waiting to be filled.

It became clear to us that we should start some sort of magazine about pets. And it came to us pretty quickly that it should be about the pets we had experience with: reptiles. As we explored the idea, we realized that a magazine would include *all* of our fields. We would have to do a lot of writing, we would be finding out about our pets, we would be educating people about their pets, and we would be passing on specialized information to people who probably wouldn't be able to get it elsewhere. As far as we could see, there was only one scientific journal on the field of reptiles: *Herpetologica,* put out by the Herpetologists' League. We discovered that there was once another magazine about reptiles and amphibians, but it failed because it was too technical for the average reader. We decided it was essential to publish something that anyone could read—anyone interested in reptiles, that is. It was at this point that we realized we had used the copycat method of finding an idea: We'd found someone doing something successfully, located a niche, and adapted it.

It was clear from the start that we'd be selling our service to individuals rather than businesses. We wanted our audience to be made up of people like us, ordinary reptile owners who wanted to know more about how to make their cold-blooded darlings happy. We went to the library and did a data base search for articles about the popularity of pets—reptiles in particular. We uncovered all sorts of facts that backed up our case. It seemed that breeding reptiles was a boom industry. There was even an article in a style magazine about lizards being the ultimate fashion accessory.

It was eleven o'clock one Saturday evening when we pieced it all together. We decided that we were going to start a magazine about raising and breeding reptiles. We pulled Iggy and Squiggy out of their terrarium, put them on the kitchen table, popped a couple of cans of premium beer, and gave them a toast. Our next step would be to further refine and test our idea, and that's the subject of the next chapter.

For more information on the topics covered in Chapter Five, take a look at the following books:

- *Great Businesses You Can Start on a Shoestring in a Recession or Depression* (Gordon, 1992)
- *How to Generate New, Original, Money-Making Ideas,* by Dean R. Mulville (American Classical, 1980)
- *Mind Your Own Business: The Best Businesses You Can Start Today for Under Five Hundred Dollars,* by Stephen Wagner and the editors of *Income Opportunities* (Adams, 1992)
- *One Hundred & Eighty-Four Businesses Anyone Can Start & Make a Lot of Money,* by Chase Revel (Bantam, 1984)
- *One Hundred & One Best Businesses to Start,* by Sharon Kahnn and Philip Lieff (Doubleday, 1992)
- *One Hundred & Sixty-Eight More Businesses Anyone Can Start & Make a Lot of Money,* by the staff of *Entrepreneur* (Bantam, 1991)
- *One Hundred Surefire Businesses You Can Start with Little or No Investment,* by Jeffrey Feinman (Jove, 1984)
- *Out of Your Mind . . . & Into the Marketplace,* by Linda Pinson and Jerry Jinnett (Out of Your Mind, 1988)
- *Starting from Scratch: 500 Profitable Business Opportunities,* by Joe S. Gould (Wiley, 1987)

⬥ 6 ⬥

THE KRAMDEN FACTOR

Testing Your Idea

Even though you've developed an idea you think will work, and have figured out who or what your customer is going to be, that doesn't mean you should jump right into the planning and fund-raising process. In order to maximize the odds of success, you should bounce your ideas off other people, including your family, friends, potential customers, and even possible competitors.

We know you're confident and eager to begin, but please take time to test your idea. Do you remember the television show "The Honeymooners"? Jackie Gleason, as Ralph Kramden, played a downtrodden bus driver. Every week he came up with ideas to strike it rich. When his wife, Alice, found out about his harebrained schemes, she would warn him they didn't make sense. Ralph never listened to her, and invariably the schemes failed, succumbing to whatever she'd warned him about. We're not implying your idea is harebrained, or even that your mate/sibling/ friend/parent is smarter than you. We're simply suggesting that you need to get outside feedback on your ideas before you go any further. It may save you some embarrassment or, more important, money. Unlike Ralph Kramden, you can't start over fresh every week.

But before you take your idea out into the world, here's a list of questions you should ask yourself:

WILL YOUR SERVICE BE SPECIAL?

Is it special because it's original? Or because you're doing it better or cheaper than someone else? There are a lot of other small businesses out there, and you need to distinguish yourself somehow.

The Advertising Partnership, the agency begun by Tony Morgan and his partners, Joe Prior and Judy Pines, works simply because they do something better than other people. The three principals are specialists in their own areas. Morgan is an expert in marketing strategies, Prior in account management and packaged goods marketing, and Pines in creative management. And instead of being separated by miles of carpeted office, they are all in touch with every project being worked on. Morgan says that while they work as a team, they don't brainstorm. "I think brainstorming is fairly useless. Groups don't come up with answers. They can implement, but they're not good for insights. At the Advertising Partnership we find that if someone knows what he or she is doing and feels strongly about it, it's usually better to go in that direction as fast as we can, rather than spending weeks deliberating."

Quick minds and imaginative, forceful responses—the qualities that make people successful at advertising—are often stifled in a corporate structure. The Partnership distinguishes itself by being flexible and personal, and unlike other start-up advertising agencies, the principals have a great deal of experience on which to base their judgments. When clients meet the partners, they know they'll be dealing with the top minds in the company for the duration of the project. They won't be shunted off to some junior associate as soon as the contract is signed.

WILL YOU PROVIDE QUALITY SERVICE?

You can't hide behind the quality of your product in a service business. It's just you and the customer. If the customer doesn't come back, you're going to use up your available pool of customers pretty quickly.

Enterprise Rent-a-Car has grown steadily since it was started in St. Louis in 1957. It grew because it made sure the customer was happy. Chris Schimpf, business manager for Brooklyn and Queens in New York City, describes the attitude of the company:

"The bottom line is customer satisfaction. We think word of mouth is better than media advertising. We know we aren't perfect. But when we have an unhappy customer, we make sure we show them that we're making an effort to give them better service. We know it works because we get a lot of referred sources. We've grown here in Brooklyn and Queens, even despite the recession."

WILL YOU PROVIDE GOOD VALUE?

During the nineties, the idea of something being a "good value" has become increasingly important. This is an aesthetic that will last well into the new century. What would you think was a fair price for your service? This may have no effect on the price you actually charge (you're probably underselling yourself), but it's good to think about it nevertheless. And of course, "good value" doesn't mean cheap.

Lewis Lipnick's business provides a service that offers good value, but at a price. Lipnick, the principal contrabassoonist for the National Symphony Orchestra, also runs "Your Silent Partner," a consultancy based in Washington, D.C., that acoustically transforms living rooms so that they sound like particular concert halls. For example, if you love the sound of music played in Carnegie Hall, then Lipnick will design a music system that can re-create that experience. Obviously this isn't a service that everyone would need or want, so Lipnick runs the risk of quickly running out of customers. However, he's found a discerning clientele, one that includes U.S. senators, top attorneys, and internationally recognized conductors. These people appreciate the sensation of sitting in a particular concert hall and are able to provide enough service to make the company work. "My service is targeted to certain people," he says. "I even tell some people I don't think this will work for them. It's for people who want to be involved with the music."

Lipnick meets with the clients and interviews them about which concert halls they like and where they prefer to sit. Then he advises them on which speakers, CD players, turntables, and tape decks they ought to buy. Finally he works with architects and interior designers to adjust the acoustics of the room so it sounds like the desired concert hall. ''There's no one else out there who knows the music like I do and who isn't selling equipment. I'm honest, I tell people what they need, I don't sell people what I have in stock. I had some clients recently who had just built a huge house. They wanted music piped into every room. They wanted 'champagne,' and I told them what it would cost. Well, they went ballistic, but I told them, 'You can't buy a Rolls-Royce for the price of a Chevy.' '' While there are other people who offer similar services, Lipnick has a technical reputation, musical knowledge, and the experience in the business, which sets him apart. He's made himself special by giving people good value for their money.

HOW DIFFICULT WILL IT BE FOR PEOPLE TO USE THIS SERVICE?

Would you want to go to the service or would you prefer that it come to you? If it's a new service, it has to be very simple to use.

That's one reason computer services like Prodigy aren't as popular as some people thought they were going to be: People aren't sure how to set them up, and it's often easier to use a phone for many of the services available. Mark Solomon, an information broker who works for a business library in New York City, puts it this way. ''People are in awe of their modems. They know there's information out there they could tap into themselves, but they think, 'Why should I pay for the privilege of making mistakes? I'll just use the telephone.' ''

WILL YOU BE ABLE TO CHANGE QUICKLY?

Opening day is just the beginning. You may have detailed plans for the next five years, but you must be able to adjust your plans if something you counted on changes. The idea is to have an enjoyable time making money, and if you need to ditch part of your original plan in order to continue doing that, so be it. You might end up working in a different market or even providing a different service.

Gavin Debecker, a former FBI agent, began running a security service for celebrities. He was doing well, but after a few years, realized he should define his business even further. He now runs a company that specializes in "threat assessment." If a movie star receives any threatening letters or telephone calls, Debecker's company analyzes them, tries to develop a profile of the person who sent the mail or made the call, and decides whether or not the threat is real.

Accounting firms and law firms often tie their services in to the changing economic and demographic patterns of the nation. Right now many law firms are expanding their elder law departments so they can deal with the problems our aging population will bring, such as nursing home care. During boom years accountants specialize in helping businesses start up. During recessions they turn around and help businesses go through bankruptcy.

WILL YOU BE COMPETING AGAINST LARGE CORPORATIONS?

If so, beware. They'll have done more preparation and will have deeper pockets than you. This means they'll be as aware as you of any potential profits to be made and will have more to spend on marketing. Worse yet, they'll be able to undercut your prices. But don't despair. What you're counting on is your ability to respond and adapt quickly. If your value and quality are top-notch, then you may be able to beat out the giants.

American Express recognized that people felt the need to have a lawyer they could turn to, even if they never actually used him or her. To capitalize on this, American Express started the Legal Services Plan. The cardholder pays $7.95 a month and is entitled to access to a "network of licensed, qualified local attorneys." This access includes unlimited phone consultations, document review, and having letters written for you. Of course, there is a scale of fixed rates for more complicated legal procedures, and the bargain varies from state to state according to local statutes. For example, the leaflet notes, "To comply with state regulations, residents of Arkansas, Indiana, Nebraska and Virginia pay $5.00 for each letter or phone call." Nevertheless, American Express has cleverly tapped into something that many people had a need for: a reliable lawyer. Another attraction is the appeal to people's vanity—always a good selling point: People like to be able to say, "I'll call my lawyer" or "I have a lawyer on retainer."

Naturally, smart consumers would think twice about having American Express choose their lawyers for them. And while the illusion of frequent communication between lawyer and the client is played up in the advertising, it's not hard to imagine just how much time a busy lawyer would want to spend chatting to a "bulk buy" customer. As a 21st Century entrepreneur, you can beat large corporations, but you need to be nimble and aware of their weaknesses. And remember, corporations need to hire actors and actresses to smile for them on TV. You can smile at your customers in person.

WILL YOU BE ABLE TO ATTRACT A TALENTED WORK FORCE?

If you plan on hiring employees, the need for a talented work force is obvious. If you're planning on a solo business, you may think the question irrelevant. But think ahead: If your business takes off, will you need other people to help you? What are you willing to offer someone who comes to work for you? He or she may get better pay elsewhere. You may need to offer other incentives. (For more information on employees, see Chapter Fourteen.)

Ruth Lambert is the CEO of Forms and Worms, a company based in New Haven, Connecticut. Forms and Worms provides specialized forms to real estate companies. Lambert says that a satisfied work force is part of her idea of what a company should be and that she chose to create a company that treats its employees in a certain way. Though she realizes that this makes the firm's products more expensive than those of some of its rivals, she wouldn't have it any other way. "We need to keep the price up to pay for the things about the company that I think are important, like day care and health coverage. We have on-site infant day care. I'm very proud of that. So far, twelve children have gone through it."

Once you've answered these eight questions yourself, it's time to turn to the other members of your family. They are your first customers: If you can't sell them on the idea, you're in big trouble. On the other hand, if you can convince them to take the journey with you (and we mean convince, not steamroll!), then you're off to a good start.

Sit down and talk. Explain what you've managed to do. If your family is opposed, then be aware this might cause problems later on when the project begins to need real financial commitment. Don't regard any hesitancy as stupidity or small-mindedness. The bankers you're going to meet later on will be even more wary. But it's not wise to go beyond the first part of this book without the support and commitment of your family. Assuming, of course, you want to stay together, and avoid factoring alimony payments into your financial plans! In L.A. County a study found that the number of divorces involving a business had doubled within a decade.

Having questioned yourself and involved your family, it's time to get out into the world and find two groups of people: your potential customers and your potential rivals. Rephrase the questions you asked yourself previously and put them to your future customers. Let the responses guide you as you continue in your search. If ten people in a row say firmly that they wouldn't pay someone to shop for their groceries, then take the hint and ask the eleventh person whether there's anything he or she would pay you to shop for.

The potential customers you interview can be from the same town or city, but when it's time to interview potential rivals, be a little more circumspect. Do your research in a locale with demographics similar to the area where you're planning to set up business, but not the same one. In a major city, ten blocks from your intended location would probably be far enough. In a small city you'd probably better do your research twenty or thirty blocks away. If you live in a small town or suburb, rent a room at a motel in another town for a couple of nights and spend a day or two interviewing people in your field of business. In a rural area, you'd probably want to do your canvassing a few counties away.

After all your thinking and research, you probably know better than your rivals how the market is going to change. But there's still a lot of useful information you can get from them. Be careful, however, not to give too much of your knowledge away. Just play excited and naive. Here are four things to find out from your rivals.

HOW MUCH DO THEY CHARGE?

You can simply call up as a customer to find this out. Ask if there are discounts for other businesses or a yearly fee for heavy users.

WHAT ARE THEIR OPERATING EXPENSES?

You'd be surprised at how much information companies will give you if you just talk away, playing the confused enthusiast. Inquire from the landlord about renting space in the same building as a rival to see what your rent might be. Go to more conferences and trade fairs and complain bitterly about your own overhead. You can be sure someone will top your tale of woe.

WHAT NEWSPAPERS AND MAGAZINES DO THEY READ?

Knowing which papers they read tells you a lot more than where they put their advertising. It tells you what information they're receiving, and even more important, what information they're not receiving.

WHAT WOULD THEY DO DIFFERENTLY IF THEY COULD START OVER?

Once again, they'll be happy to regale you with tales of what they did wrong and managed to correct. At the very least, they'll tell you about mistakes that other people have made. Some will seem obvious. Others will come as a surprise. Take heed and learn.

Analyze this information, mull it over, and answer this final question: What service business do you plan to start? Compress your answer into two short sentences. Practice saying them. Congratulations! You are now the proud owner of a workable idea.

WE PUT IGGY AND SQUIGGY TO THE TEST

Well, we felt pretty excited when we first came up with our surefire idea—the magazine about reptiles. It neatly combined our strengths—writing, teaching, and sorting information—and our main leisure activity, looking after Iggy and Squiggy. But when we put this through the Ralph Kramden test, we came up with something a little different, as you'll see. Our first stop was the list of eight questions from the beginning of this chapter.

Why was our magazine going to be special? Simply because it would be the only one available about reptiles.

Would it provide a quality service? Well, quality in a magazine has two aspects: content and look. The content would be of high quality. We could be sure of that because both of us are good researchers and we both like to write. The look of the magazine, however, we weren't so sure about. Neither of us has had any experience in design. We can't draw, although we knew we could hire someone to do that for us. We knew taking a good photo isn't as easy as it sounds. Also, there was the very basic problem of paper quality. We did some research and found that most hobby/ enthusiast magazines are printed on glossy (read "expensive") paper. Visuals seemed to count as much as text (especially in some of the less salubrious magazines!). These problems gave us our first pause. If nothing else, we'd require a lot more start-up capital.

A little disheartened, we thought about the next question: Would the magazine provide good value? Well, we could see that specialist magazines cost more than general interest magazines.

The actual amount we could charge depended on the number of advertisers we could attract—more important even than how many annual subscriptions or newsstand copies we could sell. But we had no idea what that number was. More research was obviously needed.

The next question also raised some problems: How difficult would it be for people to use this service? If people couldn't get the magazine, or didn't know it existed, they wouldn't be able to use it. We realized we had absolutely no idea about how to distribute a magazine. We supposed we could take our idea to a publisher and try to convince him or her to finance the idea. But that would be selling out too soon. This was supposed to be our project, something we created. The idea of bringing our magazine from news agent to news agent in an attempt to get them to carry it didn't seem practical or very safe, since we had heard some vaguely frightening comments about the publication distribution business.

At least we knew we could respond positively to the next question, "Will you be able to change quickly?" There were only two of us, and while we knew we'd need to plan each issue ahead a couple of months, we felt pretty confident that we could respond to the fast-moving world of the reptile.

Unfortunately, the next question was also a problem. Yes, we would definitely be competing against large corporations. We could pretty much count on the fact that if we ever started making a profit, a large publishing company would either start a copycat magazine or buy us out. The latter option might at least net us some money. The former would bankrupt us.

After all these negatives, a final positive: Locating a talented work force—that would be us—was no problem. But while we were still confident, we were beginning to recognize the gaps in our knowledge. We didn't know anything about distribution or production, or even advertising—basically, we didn't know anything about any of the practical parts of the magazine business.

We examined our problems and responses. We decided that the real problem was one of scale. We wanted to be involved in every aspect of our project, but we didn't have the experience necessary to start a magazine from scratch. Neither one of us was willing or able to go and work for a magazine and learn the business side of the operation. We wanted to start now, but what could we do?

The solution came to us one day when we were in a gourmet food store in our neighborhood. Near the register was a newsletter that described the products available in the store; it also contained recipes and bits of advice and folklore. What really caught our attention was that most of the customers were leaving the store with it under their arms.

Excited, we decided a newsletter was the solution. A newsletter would do everything a magazine would do, but wouldn't require the enormous capital outlays. We'd be involved with every aspect of production: We knew enough about computers to run simple desktop publishing programs. A neighborhood printer would be able to produce it for us. We wouldn't need to use glossy paper because it's acceptable to have a newsletter printed on ordinary paper. We could examine the going rate for newsletter subscriptions to give us an idea of pricing. We could rely on mailing lists rather than news agent distribution. And, to begin with anyway, we wouldn't need to worry about advertising—we'd concentrate on making our money from subscriptions rather than ads. We thought a newsletter wouldn't attract the attention of large corporations—we'd be too small for them to bother with and we'd be able to carve out a niche. The newsletter would also be more intimate than a magazine: It would almost be like a personal letter to friends.

Having defined our idea (or so we thought), we sat down and talked to people about a reptile newsletter. Most people hemmed and hawed: Our families were skeptical initially, but we showed them how we had arrived at the idea, and they seemed to warm up to it. Next we went to various pet store owners in our city. We asked them how reptiles had been selling. They said that next to the dog, reptiles of all sorts were the best-selling pets. We went to the suburbs around our home city and visited small-town pet stores. We persuaded friends to visit pet shops wherever they went. And, armed with a list of questions from us, they discussed pet popularity and lizard lovableness all over the country.

We knew the only other existing reptile newsletter was for

scientists, so we felt there was definitely going to be a market for our more general, somewhat humorous publication. Looking around at similar publications for other pets, we got a rough idea of how much to charge, though, of course, we weren't going to be held to that when it came to a final pricing. We called the authors of a number of different pet-related newsletters and asked about their operations—how they are set up, what sort of financing they have, and how they distribute their newsletters. We asked what the authors read, and then found and read those magazines. Most of them were happy to talk because they didn't see us as rivals. They told us all about the problems they'd had and how they had survived.

After more research we gradually began to realize something. The newsletters were divided into two types. Those that dealt with whole species—such as *Cats Now* and *Horses Today*—and those that dealt with breeds—like *Afghan Hounds and You* and *Gold Fish!* We had been planning to write the newsletter about all reptiles but began to realize how broad a topic that was. It also became clear that snake lovers really don't have much in common with lizard lovers. It was as though we were going to start a magazine about mammals and expected both whale watchers and horse breeders to buy it. We realized we had to specialize and that we should write about what we knew best: iguanas. So we asked ourselves the same series of questions, but this time with an iguana newsletter in mind. We called our newsletter *Raising Iguanas for Fun and Profit,* or *RIFP* for short.

After all this testing and redirection, we were able to condense our whole concept into two sentences: "We will publish an informative and accessible newsletter about raising and breeding iguanas. Our income will be based on subscriptions rather than advertising." And there we were, all set to move into business, but before we could start writing our first cover story, we still had some work to do. The next step was to put together a plan organizing logistics and finances. The next chapter will show you how to draft this plan, which we call the *business checklist.*

II.
PUT YOUR MONEY
WHERE YOUR
MOUTH IS

The next eight chapters are the heart of this book. These are the chapters that will help take you through the exciting and terrifying moment when you actually start to spend money. This is the point when you make the real commitment and actually become an entrepreneur rather than a well-prepared dreamer.

THE BUSINESS CHECKLIST

Raising Iguanas for Fun and Profit

Traditionally, what you would do next is write a business plan. There's an entire industry devoted to business plans: Countless books and articles are written every year on the subject. Many people actually make a living preparing such plans for new businesses—which we feel is like paying someone to take your driving test. Business plans are daunting, they seem complex and involve a lot of research, but they are essential. They make you think carefully about what you're getting into and what you need to prepare for.

When we asked Greg Heisler, the photographer, whether he had any kind of business plan when he started, he laughed. "No, I was a happy little kid, playing. I had no plan at all. I was too busy and never had any idea about how to run a business. If I ever had a choice of doing paperwork and sending out bills, or being flown to California on assignment for *Life,* I always chose to fly off." How did he solve this problem? "I got married! I came back here with my wife, Wendy Bryan, from Australia, and she looked at the mess, all the receipts in shoe boxes, and said, 'Jeez, I've entrusted my life to you?' She basically rolled up her sleeves and dove in. Actually, when she came along, I was almost broke—despite working all the time. I had terrible cash flow. I never understood that I was in business. I thought it was a hobby."

You can't rely on someone to come along and save you at the last moment—you've got to know what's going on from day one. However, as a 21st Century entrepreneur, you aren't going to need to write a formal business plan . . . at least not at this point. Instead, you'll be developing what we call a business checklist.

This is what it will look like:

Chapter	Task	Date Begun	Date Completed
7	Choosing your company name	_____	_____
7	Choosing your company philosophy	_____	_____
8	Choosing location	_____	_____
9	Calculating start-up costs	_____	_____
10	Calculating fees	_____	_____
10	Calculating working capital	_____	_____
11	Finding seed money	_____	_____
12	Getting your clients' attention	_____	_____
13	Keeping your clients' attention	_____	_____
14	Finding people to work for you	_____	_____

For each of these tasks you should make a file. As we go through the next eight chapters, you'll gradually fill each file with all your calculations and notes, creating a flexible 21st Century version of a business plan.

In order to understand why we're suggesting you abandon the traditional route, let's take a look at the typical role of the business plan. It serves two purposes. First, it shows banks you've thought out your business so they'll be persuaded to lend you money. Second, it forces you to map out your business so you know where you're going. For most people reading this book, only the second reason is relevant because, to start with anyway, no bank is going to lend you money. Sure, you've seen all the ads about your friendly local banker wanting to help out struggling businesses. Bunkum. The loan officer at your local bank is more likely to lend ten thousand dollars to a drug dealer than she is to you. In her eyes, the drug dealer's much more likely to make a profit. Of course, if you run your business successfully for a couple of years, the banks will beg to lend you money. Then they'll probably ask you to appear in a commercial declaring how much they helped you. Until then, you're better off looking for other sources of finance (which we will go over in Chapter Eleven).

While you won't be using it to obtain financing, your business checklist will fulfill the second, and we believe more important, role of a business plan: providing you with a map for your future business success. Of course, since it is entirely an internal document, the business checklist will be less formal than the traditional plan. You won't need to type it out and put it in a binder, and you won't need to follow a strict formula—just address the problems we discuss in Chapters Seven through Fourteen and keep your notes together. The final product will offer you an idea of what you're going to be doing for the next five years. Even though your ideas will change as you progress, it's always good to have something to refer back to. Best of all, if you do eventually need a formal business plan, all the groundwork will be there. You can go back and rework it into the traditional format.

YOUR COMPANY PHILOSOPHY

The first task is to name your company. Choose a catchy name that lets your potential customers know immediately what service you're offering. Live with it for a week or two before you make a final decision—what seems clever one day may seem ridiculous the next. Avoid the enigmatic—Integrated Resources sounds like an important name, but it could as easily be a recycling company as a temp agency.

The next task is to write a company philosophy. This will set out how you intend to work with your suppliers, customers, and workers. Look back at the brief description of the business you wrote at the end of Chapter Six. Now expand on that. Decide what business you're in. That's not always as simple a question as you may think. Rolls-Royce, for instance, doesn't sell cars, it sells class, wealth, and luxury. Other companies sell cars that are just as comfortable and expensive, but Rolls-Royce stands above them because it can rely on excellent word of mouth and its reputation. You rarely see them advertising on TV.

Put down in writing what the soul of your company is going to be. Don't think that just because you're currently the only employee, it's always going to be that way. You must create a philosophy that you'll be able to live with and that can inspire you, your employees, and your customers. Be specific: Promise to return all your calls the day they come in, for example. Promise that you'll make a point to remember the names of your customers' children. When you've finished, type it out neatly, buy a decent frame, and hang it above your telephone. And refer to it constantly. It will serve as your conscience on those days you think that running a business is only about making money.

At Enterprise Rent-a-Car, posted on the wall where the customer waits to pick up the car, is a paragraph entitled "What is a customer?" This is Enterprise's statement of how it will deal with its clients. "Everyone at Enterprise knows the customer is important, and customers stand there and read it," says Chris Schimpf. "I don't know what direct effect it has, but I think it must seep into the customers' minds. I know for a fact a lot of people like it so much, they've asked if they can get it for their own companies."

Of course, we wrote out a business philosophy for *RIFP*. At first, to be honest, we wondered whether it was really worth our effort. We weren't like a car-rental company—we didn't plan to have much personal contact with our customers. As long as the newsletter arrived on time, how much philosophy did we need? Well, as it turned out, our plans evolved and we did frequently end up talking with our customers. We also found that the philosophy really kept us focused, both during the planning stages and afterwards. The two-line description of our business was: "We will publish an informative and accessible newsletter about raising and breeding iguanas. Our income will be based on subscriptions rather than advertising." That was fair enough, but we needed to explore the idea more for our philosophy.

What business were we really in? What were we selling? On the face of it, we were selling information about iguanas. But if a customer wanted that, he could talk to a vet or pick up a book. We were selling more than information. We would be giving people peace of mind and a feeling of community. They would know they were doing right by their reptiles and that there were other people out there with odd pets like theirs. It's not as though you'll meet all the other iguana owners out walking their pets in the park every morning. We'd help the owners understand what is normal behavior for an iguana. Dog owners can talk and are able to comfort and inform one another with a reassuring "Oh yes, my dog always does that."

After many rough drafts, we came up with this: "At *RIFP* we understand that iguanas have their own needs and problems. Our job is to help owners to understand the nature of the iguana and how to provide their pets with the best possible living environment outside the iguana's natural habitat. We will do this with clearly written, short articles about everyday subjects of interest to the owners of iguanas. We will choose articles and stories based on the responses we get from our readers. We will reply within a week to each letter written to us with either the information requested or suggestions about where to find the answer. We will keep a record of information about each subscriber's pet. For example, the name and breed of the iguana, place of purchase, and so on. This will allow us to personalize our responses. We will always present ourselves as the self-taught equals of our readers—we're enthusiasts, not experts. And last but not least, we will always keep our sense of humor.'' We printed this philosophy on good-quality paper and bought a frame to put it in. It's amazing, but talking about it and writing it down and framing it made us feel ready to take on anything.

YOUR COMPANY PHILOSOPHY

At _____ we will: *(define the soul of your product here)* _____

_____ .

We will do this through *(define the means through which you will do business here)* _____

_____ .

To ensure good client relations, we will _____

_____ .

We will present ourselves as _____

_____ .

Last, but not least _____

_____ .

Armed with a calculator, many pads of paper, and a packet of pencils, we were ready to start our business checklist. Our next task, and yours, is to decide where the business should be based: at home or in an office.

❖ 8 ❖

JUGGLING CHAIN SAWS

Where Should Your Business Be Located?

I t used to be easy to decide where you wanted your business to be based: You went where everybody else went. For example, if you were a financier in New York City, you rented a suite on Wall Street. If you were in advertising, you made sure you had a Madison Avenue address. If you were a doctor, you looked for a place on Park Avenue. If you sold flowers, you needed a shop in the flower district; if you sold diamonds, you needed a shop in the diamond district on Forty-eighth Street. And while Manhattan is unusual in that, because of its size and uniquely commercial orientation, it has more of these specialized districts than most cities, the same sort of strict location guidelines have held true for most American towns and cities. This is an interesting tradition left over from the Middle Ages in Europe, when you would have found all the silversmiths working alongside one another, and all the butchers grouped together on another street. The advantages to such a formalized plan are that it allows for the businesses to have ready access to vendors and resources, and it makes it easy for clients to comparison-shop—theoretically they can go door to door looking for exactly what they need.

Those advantages still hold true for retailers and manufacturers, but not for service businesses, although there may be a little prestige in having your business in a particular area. But if you pay too much for prestigious floor space, you're not getting your business off to a good start. You're also probably losing potential customers who wonder why they should subsidize your fancy offices. You can't go into the 21st Century making assumptions and relying on tradition, and choice of location is one of the most important decisions you'll be making.

We like to think of doing business in the 21st Century as juggling chain saws—large, ten-horsepower, monster chain saws. One chain saw has "business commitments" printed on its side, while the other is labeled "family commitments." For the 21st Century entrepreneur, life-style is as important as business success. For many, in fact, the quest for a better life-style is what drove them to become an entrepreneur. To ensure a healthy business and a decent life-style, you'll need to keep juggling these two chain saws steadily and carefully, for many years. If you lose control of one, the consequences will be disastrous—you may lose an arm and a leg. You have two choices as a service-business entrepreneur. You can either learn how to juggle chain saws yourself, in which case you'll be working out of your home, or you can pay someone else to juggle for you, in which case you'll be working from an office, loft, or storefront outside your home. Let's look more closely at these two options.

It would appear to make more sense to let someone else juggle those chain saws. A landlord can relieve you of some of the stress associated with the business. Landlords are the ones who need to fix the roof and clean up the flood in the basement and arrange for garbage disposal. But think about it for a second. You are going to pay this person a lot for his time. The money spent on renting an empty room may have been better spent on developing your business. In order to decide whether or not it makes sense to pay a landlord, we suggest you focus on how you and your clients will be meeting. Generally, either clients will be coming to you, or you will be going to them. While there are exceptions to the rule, if clients will be coming to you, rent an office; if you will be going to them, we think you should work from your home.

RENTING AN OFFICE

Let's look at what makes a good location. For some businesses you really do need a location with good customer traffic, accessibility, and visibility—all the qualities usually associated with a retail store. An example of this would be a repair service, like a cobbler or clock mender, which should be located on the way to something else. Most people can't be bothered to go out of their way just to drop off one pair of shoes, but are perfectly happy to do it on the way to the supermarket or the train station. Rental businesses should also be well situated. A bicycle-rental store near a park will do a lot more business than one next to a freeway.

IF YOU NEED HIGH VISIBILITY

If you need a business location with high visibility, then you must choose between a shopping mall or a main street. One advantage of renting on a main street is that you can really attract the attention of passersby. Your signs and store windows have more impact than they would in a mall, where the stores tend to look alike. You can also expand next door more easily should the opportunity or need arise. However, the disadvantage of a main street location is that you may not be able to attract as much foot traffic.

All malls are not equal: Some are just clusters of convenience stores in a cul-de-sac, or mini-malls. These can be great places for small service businesses, as long as the neighborhood knows you're there. For example, a video-rental store or a dry cleaner will draw customers from the immediate neighborhood. Larger, more traditional malls will draw people from all over the community and thus increase foot traffic, but they'll also take more money out of your pocket in rent. You'll also be bound by more bylaws and probably need to pay contributions to the mall's upkeep and advertising.

Within a larger mall, it's crucial that you have a say in where your business is located. After all, a business that repairs household appliances would lose out if it were situated next to a shop that sold new appliances: Customers would think, "I'll just buy a new one." (Of course, if you were an extraordinary marketer, you could turn this disadvantage around by selling reconditioned models to those who were turned off by the high prices next door.) You may want to have it written into your lease that no competitors will be allowed to set up shop too close to you. It's okay for a lot of shoe stores or jewelers to be near one another: There's enough variety to actually encourage people to go from one store to the next. But if you're renting videos, you don't want to open the shop one day and see Blockbuster Video signs going up across the way.

You should always try to find out exactly who comes to the mall or main street to shop. You can ask mall owners for specifics and then check it out yourself. On a main street you'll need to rely more on your own observations. Landlords love to talk about how gentrified certain run-down areas are becoming. Don't be blinded by your love for a site. If the neighborhood looks like a dump, it is a dump. Don't believe the talk about the new city buildings being built across the road or planned parks until you actually see them. More established stores can afford to take a risk, but you'll need to forgo the cheaper rents to obtain the security of a fairly established location.

Gentrification is in the eye of the beholder. Real estate agents and landlords tend to be more optimistic than residents. Frequently, upscale shops will creep up a shopping street during the good years, and then retreat when times get tough. You don't want to be a pioneer in a changing neighborhood, because you may be left with a high-rent lease in what has reverted to a low-rent area. Make sure you walk all around your new neighborhood and look at new and closed stores. Ask your landlord and your neighbors what the turnover has been in the store you're renting.

Accessibility is very important. If you live in a town with public transportation, make sure you're near a station or stop. The ideal would be to rent a space on one of the streets that people walk by on their way to the station. Main roads can be good locations, but make sure the buses stop on your side of the street. If there's a median, make sure that pedestrians can (and actually do) cross from one side to the other. If possible, pay a little more and get a corner site—you'll attract customers from both streets, maybe even doubling your foot traffic. Finally, check whether you're on the sunny side of the street. In the winter people walk down that side; in the summer they walk down the other side. If you have a business that's seasonal, this might be important.

IF YOU DON'T NEED TO BE SEEN

If there's no way you can use part of your home as an office, even if you'll be going to your customers, then you'll need to rent an office. However, in this case it's more important that your office be convenient for you rather than the customer. You need to be able to get to your office—and from there to your clients—easily. Consider how you're going to be moving around. Will it be by car? Then you'll need safe parking near your office and access to a main road. Will you be traveling by public transportation? In that case, make sure that the routes that pass by your office also go where you think your customers will be.

THE RENTAL AGREEMENT

Before you sign a lease, go to a real estate lawyer and discuss it. It'll cost you, but you will have factored this expense into your start-up costs (see Chapter Nine). Rest assured, it will be money well spent. Most leases are heavily stacked against tenants, and you need all the help you can get.

For a start, your real estate lawyer will be able to help you deal with your broker. Remember that a broker's primary relationship is with the landlord. Once you've signed and the commission has been paid, you're essentially out of the broker's life. The landlord's other properties are still there for the real estate broker to profit from. So, while brokers can help a little in negotiating a price, they aren't really the friends they pretend they are. With luck you'll find a broker who's honest and will get you the best deal possible, but you can't hope for more than that.

Your lawyer is being paid to do most of the work, but you should know a few things about the lease. The lease you sign should be short term but should also have renewal options that stretch at least as far as your estimated break-even point (see Chapter Ten). This gives you great flexibility. You can commit or quit as your business needs dictate, rather than as your lease commands. Your lease should also extend as long as your loans so your investors will see you have confidence in your business. Also, being in one place for a long time will build up customer loyalty.

Don't trust your landlord. It's nothing personal, it's just that he or she is in business, the same as you. Landlords want as much as possible out of the deal, and they probably know more loopholes than you do. (Such an understanding attitude is easy when you're writing about the topic. It's harder to remain calm if you find out you've been paying to heat the basement your landlord's son uses to practice the drums on Saturday afternoons.) Here are some suggestions about your lease negotiations:

- Watch out for what are known as "pass-alongs." Landlords are allowed to assess for items like lobby areas, air-conditioning, heating, taxes, and insurance. Make sure that you're not paying more than your fair share.
- Try to get your landlord to help you out financially. Persuade him or her to pick up any renovation costs. It might actually be better to pay a little more every month if the landlord has paid for the work to be done. If you need to make the renovations, this means getting together more money up front to pay for it. By paying for the work as part of the rent, you'll be spreading the cost out over a few years.
- See whether you can get your landlord to make any rent concessions. It's important for a landlord to make sure his properties are occupied: If your landlord owns a number of adjacent stores that are empty, he or she will be eager to create the impression of a thriving commercial site, and your business can help do that. Ask for three months free rent to begin with; you may just get it.
- Ask that the deposit be waived. Instead, offer a promissory note or a personal guarantee from a relative. This would free up some of your scarce money.
- If you decide to incorporate (we will go over the advantages and disadvantages of this in Chapter Nine), make sure it's the corporation, not you, that signs the lease.
- Are you getting what you're paying for? Don't be embarrassed about getting down on your hands and knees and measuring the space that's actually usable. Don't pay for the space taken up by pillars.
- While it's not pleasant to consider, you may need to eventu-

ally shut up shop, so you should pay careful attention to the "assignability" of your lease. If you can assign the lease, it means that you can sell it or sublet the space. You should also request that the lease allow the location to be used for "any legal use" or for "general use" by a business similar to yours. That way, if you have to stop business, you won't have to pay rent on an empty store.

- In addition to assignability, you can ask for "exclusivity." That means that while you're there, the landlord won't be allowed to rent to any business like yours in the same building.

- Find out exactly what rights the landlord has in terms of canceling the lease. You'll want to ask for specific reasons, appropriate compensation, and adequate time in which to respond to any accusations.

- Similarly, find out about rent increases: When will they come? How much will they be, and will you be given a reason for them?

- Speaking of rent, don't pay any until the space is renovated by the date agreed to. You should be able to cancel the lease if the landlord doesn't meet any of the conditions made.

- If you don't think you can afford the rent requested, talk to the landlord about a "graduated" rent. A graduated rent allows you to pay low rent to begin with and then more later on when, presumably, you're better off. This may be particularly attractive to a landlord in today's economic climate when an empty store can put off other potential store owners.

- Even in a good economy you can generally negotiate about ten percent off the asking rent.

You should also find out about any business incubators in your area. Run by development agencies and local governments, they consist of buildings where start-up business can share some facilities and so cut their running costs. Your local Small Business Administration should be able to put you in touch with the one nearest you.

HOME-BASED BUSINESSES

Perhaps you feel comfortable juggling your chain saws in your own house. You'll find there are a number of advantages and disadvantages, but we believe that, all in all, it's the ideal way to go for most service businesses. It's also where we decided to start our newsletter, *RIFP*.

Working outside of the home only became customary during the Industrial Revolution. Before then, you worked wherever it was most convenient. Many people lived above their businesses. However, with the advent of mass production and mills and factories, it made more sense for owners to put all the machinery under one big roof and let the workers find their own houses.

Take, for example, a woman who knitted sweaters for a living before the invention of the factory loom. She would work at home and sell the sweaters from her house or at a market or to a store. But with the advent of the loom, which could make sweaters more cheaply and faster than she could, the woman was out of business. She couldn't compete. A century later, her great-granddaughter decides she wants to go into business. Using the new home knitting machines, she can set up a designer sweater business in her house. She can make a profit because, unlike the mass-produced ones made in the big factories that drove her great-grandmother out of business, her sweaters are handmade. Since they're one of a kind, she can charge more for them and therefore compete effectively.

There's been a similar shift in the world of information. In the middle of the 20th Century, office workers were herded together into larger and larger office buildings (essentially information factories). Now they are leaving these factories to go back to work in their homes, taking their portable computers and modems with them. The huge office towers in our big cities will one day be thought of as peculiar relics, like the castles from the crusades in Europe or the pyramids in Egypt.

Why are we so convinced of the demise of the office tower? Well, first consider home employment from the corporation's perspective: When an employee's job is essentially keying information into a computer and retrieving more information from a data base located in the building's basement or even in another state, it doesn't make a lot of sense for the employee to be sitting on real estate worth thirty dollars a square foot when he or she could be working at home.

Next, think about how the basis of wealth, and therefore power, in the 21st Century will be the selling of information rather than the selling of products. Of course, manufacturing and retailing will still make up large parts of the economy, but instead of valuing material possessions, people will value information. Sometimes it'll be information valued for its own sake, like gossip; at other times it'll be information about material things, like where to get the best deal on a new television. We can foresee a time when people will brag about their new data bases rather than their new BMWs at cocktail parties.

Along with this, more transactions are going to take place using electricity instead of paper. Paper will still exist, but it will be used as a backup, not the primary mode of transactions. Our children will (for better or worse) have more faith in the backup on the hard disk than a flimsy piece of rolled tree. We have less faith than they do: We still need to touch something to believe it exists.

This transformation from information factory to home work space isn't going to happen overnight, but the evidence indicates it will happen. In 1992, according to Faith Popcorn, ''around sixteen million corporate employees worked at home either part- or full-time.'' There are also around ten million self-employed Americans who work out of their homes. If you add together the employees and entrepreneurs, you have twenty-six million people, or almost a quarter of the American work force, working from their homes.

The shift to home employment and entrepreneurship mirrors an attitudinal shift taking place in the work force. As the 21st Century approaches, people want to become more in control of their lives. The recent round of corporate layoffs has made us aware that we can't rely on large companies to care for us from graduation to retirement and that we're going to need to take responsibility for the course of our own careers. It used to be that the company you worked for identified you completely. You were an IBM man or an Avon lady. That's no longer true. Entrepreneurship, particularly home-based entrepreneurship, became sexy, partially because it allowed you to escape the identification with a company and take charge of your own life.

And as the concept gains more and more adherents, the previous prejudice against home businesses is disappearing. People who work from home are no longer thought of as unprofessional. They're considered savvy. You do need to work harder than someone with an office to present a professional image, but we'll tell you how to do that. The upshot is that no one will disrespect you for trying to make it on your own. They may try and bully you because you're a small business, but that would happen even if you had an office in a prime location.

Let's look at some of the specific advantages of a home location:

IT OFFERS A GREAT ESCAPE

We've always found working in offices stultifying. They are, after all, nothing more than sophisticated factories. There's no privacy; the air is lousy, the coffee vile, and the decor usually tasteless. And, let's face it, your friends have been chosen by the personnel department. You could do with a change. We were really looking forward to doing things our way.

IT'S CHEAPER

There you go! By simply starting your business at home, you've saved yourself one thousand dollars a month, or whatever renting a back room in an ugly office building costs. This is one thousand dollars that can be used each month for something useful . . . like advertising. We certainly needed to save all the money we possibly could, and the office in the home seemed an ideal way to begin doing that.

YOU'LL BE ABLE TO CHOOSE YOUR WORK MATES

To begin with, you may have no one working with you, but if it does happen, you'll be able to choose them because you like

them, not because the personnel department does. We were stuck
with each other, of course. We were a little nervous but decided
that we'd already chosen each other, so we might as well make
the best of it.

IT'S SIMPLER THAN RENTING

Sure, you still must deal with the taxes and insurance, and
maybe your landlord if you rent your home, but you won't be
dealing with another landlord, lease, and real estate lawyer. (And,
as we all know, the fewer lawyers, the better.)

YOU WON'T NEED TO COMMUTE

Just add up what you spend on travel every year. Even if you
already own a car, you'll love the savings on gas and maintenance,
not to mention all that time you won't be spending in traffic jams.
We realized we could actually sell our car now, since we'd only
been using it for commuting. That saved us even more money.

IT WILL HAVE BETTER AESTHETICS

Just like everyone else, you know you're the only person with
taste and discretion when it comes to pictures and furniture. Freed
from the confines of the typical office, you can finally create your
own environment: Stainless steel shelves with a lime green trim?
A year's worth of *Playgirl* centerfolds in gilt frames? Go
ahead—it's your office. (Just be careful to take the hunks down
if you ever invite customers around.) We chose some tasteful
posters from the Museum of Modern Art, framed in old gilt frames
from a flea market. They look *très* chic. And while we're on the
subject of aesthetics, what about music? In your home you'll be
free from the tyranny of Muzak, Lite Radio, Classic Rock, or
whatever percolates through your current office. You'll be able
to replace it with what you want to hear: Muzak, Lite Radio,
Classic Rock, or whatever. We compromise by playing nothing
or retreating to our headphones if one of us gets an urge to listen
to the Clash or the Psychedelic Furs.

IT CAN BE MORE EFFICIENT

If you conduct most of your business by modem or fax, over the telephone, or through the mail, then working from home makes an incredible amount of sense: Why pay for office space that no one but you will ever see? Your business's personality will exist only over the telephone lines. We didn't plan on having too many lizard lovers visiting, so this was another point in favor of a home base for *RIFP*.

IT AFFORDS YOU GREATER FREEDOM

You'll no longer suffer from the time constraints of an office. If you want to work from noon to 8:00 P.M., you can. Both of us like to get up early and go to bed early. We tend to be asleep by 10:00 P.M., but that's our preference. You want to go to Venice in the fall? So go. You don't need to check with your boss and you won't need to schedule yourself around a co-worker. We worried we'd never be able to get away for a vacation together, but decided that we could either prepare an entire issue in advance and have someone else send it out or do a double issue. (Then we realized we wouldn't be able to afford to go anywhere for a few years anyway.)

IT WILL LET US BE CLOSE TO OUR IGUANAS

In the past we've found ourselves restless and unable to concentrate by the end of the day because we're worried about our iguanas. Are they too cold? Do they have enough water? Questions like this will never bother us again when we're right there to look after them.

Even though we're strongly in favor of the home location, there are some definite disadvantages you need to factor into your decision. But since we're biased, we've also offered some solutions.

IT CAN BE TOUGH TO FIND ADEQUATE SPACE

Very few of us have an extra room lying around the house. But don't despair if you look at your shoe-box apartment and can't see an office there: You'll be amazed at what a secondhand filing cabinet and a desk can do for a corner. You should probably at least try to give yourself a room with a view, or at least a window. If we lean backwards in our chairs, we can see out the window. If we stretch far enough, we can even see some trees.

THE TELEPHONE RINGS CONSTANTLY

Well, this is actually one of those good problems to have: You'd be in real trouble if the phone didn't ring at all. However, you really do need to sort something out here. Having two phone lines—one for your family and one for your business—is probably a good idea. Just make sure that ne'er the twain shall meet. (We know of one doctor's son who was regularly asked to give his medical opinion whenever he answered the phone.) There are other solutions: During certain periods of the day, don't answer the phone. You can check your messages after a couple of hours and answer the more urgent calls right away.

However you deal with this issue, you do need a reliable answering machine with a simple, professional message. Call yourself a few times to see if the message projects the right image for your company. If you want real efficiency, use an answering service. It's up to you to decide whether it should be the automated kind or one where actual humans answer. If you choose humans, call them regularly to check on the quality of the service. You don't want someone snapping gum in the ear of a potential client. At *RIFP* we went for the cheaper option of an answering machine. We weren't planning on too much telephone communication with our subscribers to begin with. We toyed with recording part of a Godzilla movie onto the tape, but decided to take our own advice and play it safe.

IT'S PROBABLY ILLEGAL

Operating a business probably goes against your local zoning laws and it probably breaks your lease or bylaws. You should ask your lawyer to check the local home occupation laws. The definition of *home occupation* changes from state to state and from year to year. (Of course, plenty of people ignore this issue. It's your call.)

YOU MAY LOSE TOUCH WITH DEVELOPMENTS IN YOUR FIELD

Think about this carefully. If you are trying to market yourself as an expert, it's essential you remain an up-to-date expert. Magazines, newsletters, and newspapers are a good starting point, but you really need personal contact with your rivals and peers in the field. Conferences, national and local, are important, as are the computer bulletin boards you may have tapped into while researching your idea. Lunch will become a critical meal for you—try to meet people to discuss work at least twice a week.

Gregg Trueman, who works from his home, makes a conscious effort to stay aware of new developments in the field of computer design. ''I've been teaching courses at the Kodak Center for Creative Imaging in Maine. I'm educating myself as I go along. When some type of new design software comes along, I ask the school if they would let me teach a course on the topic. I call up the software company, say I'm teaching a course in the new program, and ask if they could please send me the software and any tutorial programs they have. They invariably agree since their goal is to promote use of the software.''

We planned on keeping on top of the latest research by reading books and articles in animal magazines. From time to time we planned to interview reptile experts and to get their opinions on iguanas.

YOU COULD BECOME OBSESSED

When does motivation become obsession? Only you and your family will know. If you don't have an immediate family, get some kind of surrogate family (like the members of your softball team) to give you feedback. Perspective is essential to the 21st Century entrepreneur, and if you find yourself working eighteen hours a day, five days a week, for six months, then something is wrong. Remember you're working to provide a living for yourself and your family. This was obviously going to be a danger for us; after all, we were living, breathing, and (almost) sleeping iguanas. We made our friends promise to tell us if we talked too much about Iggy and Squiggy and the newsletter. We also swore to get out and mingle with mammals frequently.

YOU COULD BECOME LONELY

Substitute the word "loneliness" for "obsession" in the paragraph above. Anna Walker found working alone to be a problem. "Ultimately I found the hardest thing about starting my own business was the solitude. I was going crazy at home all the time. One reason I started to enjoy taking my book around was that I got to see people." You must make an effort to talk to people who aren't connected to your work. Don't think that chatting on the phone during work hours is a substitute for meeting real live people; it merely wastes your time and ties up the phone.

If you have a family, make a commitment and go out and do things with them in the evenings once or twice a week or on the weekend. These trips don't need to be expensive: driving around with your children, flying a kite with your spouse, or walking in the country with your parents can be as relaxing as any prepackaged entertainment like going to the movies. If you don't have a family, you must try even harder to keep up with your circle of friends. If you didn't hold parties, start doing so. And make sure you go to all the parties you're invited to. If you don't belong to some kind of health club, then join one. Getting involved in a game or class of some sort is usually better than working out on machines because people talk more. A tennis or racquetball league is a great way to meet people. You may not like your partner much after you lose three games in a row, but at least you'll have been talking to someone else.

YOU CAN'T INVITE CLIENTS TO YOUR OFFICE

You may not be able to invite customers to your office because it's so tiny, so messy, or so full of diapers. So, again, join a local health club with a café or talk to the owner of your favorite restaurant and ask whether he'll reserve a table for you regularly. You just need somewhere quiet and understated, with comfortable chairs and a table. Look in the yellow pages for places that rent offices for the day. One lawyer we know began his business out of his home and, lacking a suitable place to meet people, used hotel lobbies. When he wanted to meet a client, he'd say, "Well, I'm going to be in midtown this afternoon. I could meet you in the lobby of the Algonquin at three. I'll be on the left as you walk in." And there he would be, sitting as though he owned the place, left to his own devices by the hotel staff.

Just as it takes you a while to get used to working in a new office, so it will take a while for you to get used to working from home. We've spoken with entrepreneurs who have successfully made the shift from information factory to home office and asked what tips they could offer those who are about to follow them. Here are their suggestions:

ESTABLISH RITUALS

Rituals are a good thing, in moderation. You certainly want to get into the habit of waking up early. Go down to the local diner and get some coffee if that makes you feel better. Try to maintain a regular daily schedule; you'll find projects don't bloat so easily if you're spending a finite time on them every day.

STAY ON TOP OF YOUR TAXES

Working from home does affect your taxes greatly. While your accountant will work out the details, you need to be aware of the basics. You can deduct a home office if it's an entire room—or partitioned area—that's used regularly and exclusively as an office. That means no kitchen tables. You'll be able to deduct a percentage of your home mortgage or rent and your utilities as well as your other expenses. Your exact tax liability will depend on the legal structure of your business—corporations are taxed differently from partnerships and sole proprietorships. Whatever the case, you'll need to keep excellent financial records, and remember that the government condones tax avoidance (legally minimizing your taxes) but prosecutes tax evasion.

"Taxes took me a long time to figure out," says Anna Walker. "It's especially hard for a free-lancer. At first it's hard to get a handle on the money you owe to the government. You must have a system. When you get a check for five hundred dollars, it's up to you to realize that you haven't just made five hundred dollars. I've found it very helpful to put aside every third check or so in a separate bank account. The only checks I write on it are for taxes."

BE REALISTIC ABOUT CHILD CARE

Don't kid yourself. You can't do two jobs at once. No one can run a successful business and look after children at the same time. You must arrange for some kind of child care, either in your house or at a center. If you opt for in-house child care, make sure your baby-sitter knows you mustn't be disturbed. Don't let yourself be distracted when you hear your beloved (or the baby-sitter) crying. A thick door will help isolate you. After a while your child will learn that the closed door means you're as far from reach as if you had driven away in a car.

BUY A GOOD CHAIR

One thing you shouldn't stint on is a decent chair. You can buy it secondhand, but make sure it adjusts and is comfortable: You're going to be spending the next few years in it.

SET GOALS AND DEADLINES

You must be your own boss breathing down your own neck (an unpleasant thought). You'll need to organize your time. Have a planner on your wall and keep one in your briefcase. Make sure the information matches.

REMEMBER TO EXPLOIT THE ADVANTAGES OF WORKING AT HOME

Give yourself a break every now and again (once a month, not once a week). Take the afternoon off and watch soap operas. Call in sick if you're sick. Read a chapter of *Pride and Prejudice* every day. Try to have some fun.

If the two chain saws you're juggling, "family commitments" and "business commitments," are important to you, then you might as well get completely involved in them. So, if you can do it, we recommend you start your business in your home. Start slowly, concentrate, and don't let your eyes wander for a second from either your family or your business. Eventually you'll find you can relax a little and look around while you're doing work . . . and maybe even enjoy the view.

Opening day is drawing closer. Now that you have a place to work, you should consider how you're going to attract customers and clients.

For more information on the topics covered in Chapter Eight, take a look at the following books:

- *Insider Home Business Riches,* by John Collins (Lion, 1989)
- *Working From Home,* by Paul and Sarah Edwards (St. Martin's, 1985)
- *The Home Office Book,* by Mark Alvarez (Goodwood, 1990)

⤞ 9 ⤝

FIRST-STEP FINANCES

How Much Will It Cost to Get Started?

Estimating how much money you need to start your business is difficult and frustrating. It always takes longer than you think. You're never sure if the numbers you're dealing with are accurate. And, to a large extent, you're at the mercy of other people. As we sat at the kitchen table planning our newsletter, *RIFP,* one of us invariably started wondering whether it was worth all the trouble.

Nonetheless, this whole procedure of estimating the money you need is fundamental to the future health of your business. The number one reason small businesses fail is that *they don't have enough money to fall back on.* No surprise there, but every year thousands of entrepreneurs relearn this lesson the hard way.

You have a specific destination in mind—profitability. You wouldn't attempt to get across the country with only a couple of dollars in your pocket. The same holds true with money for starting service businesses. You need it, a lot of it. Not as much money as you'd need for a retail business, mind you, and certainly not as much as wholesalers or manufacturers need, but as Pepsi said, "You gotta have it."

This chapter has two main sections. First you'll work out how much money you'll need to live on while you get the business going. Then you'll estimate all the onetime start-up costs you're going to have for your business. In the next chapter you'll work out how much money the business will need to live on until it breaks even. You won't actually have to spend any money yet, you're just working out what you need.

DAILY EXPENSES:
WHAT YOU WILL LIVE ON

This is the money you're going to be living on while the business takes off. It's separate from your business money and should remain that way, unless you want to end up on the street. There are three potential sources for living expenses: your spouse's wages, your savings, or your wages from another job you hold down while launching your new business on the side. But before we examine those options, we need to see how much money you'll actually require. You should draw up a list of possible expenses. The list below is just a start: You'll have many additions of your own. Look through your credit card bills, bank records, and canceled checks for the past six months to give yourself a more accurate estimate.

Mortgage or rent payment   _____
Debt service   _____
Tax payment   _____
Insurance   _____
Utilities   _____
Telephone   _____
Household maintenance   _____
Nonreimbursable medical   _____
Auto   _____
Food   _____
Entertainment   _____
Total monthly expenses   _____
Less possible part-time income   _____

Most people can tell whether their business is going to work after six months, but it could be another year or so beyond that before you actually start making money. Initially plan on carrying the preceding monthly costs for about 10 months. In the next chapter we'll show you how to estimate how long it'll take before you break even. Add to your 10-month total any once-a-year costs you'll incur like credit card fees and small birthday presents. Similarly, try to factor in any increases you can foresee, like rent increases or tax hikes. Be conservative in your estimates. It's better to be pleasantly surprised and find money left over than it is to find yourself stranded without a penny.

Obviously you should do all you can to cut down these expenses. If you have a family, you'll need to pull together. You won't want to alarm your children, but you should make them aware that until the business gets off the ground, things are going to be a little harder. Who knows? They may enjoy the excitement and the feeling that they are contributing to something that the family is doing. The important thing to remember is that you must set a realistic budget and stick to it. Everyone has different priorities, of course, but decide what you need and what you can do without. Then do without it.

Let's take a look at some of the things you can do to trim expenses. If you're like us, you'll be able to come up with some big savings if you stop eating out and ordering in. It does take more effort to make your own food, and you'll be dead tired some days, but it's an obvious and necessary sacrifice. Also, your wardrobe may need to slip out of fashion. Even if you'll need to cut a sophisticated image with clients, that doesn't mean you need to jump into every new fashion trend. Traditional business garb rarely goes out of style, so when in doubt, buy stodgy. If you have a family, they may need to make similar life-style sacrifices. Teenagers can get jobs if they want a new pair of slashed jeans or a newly released compact disk. Don't use your car unless you need to. Walk or use public transportation if you possibly can. Do some quick calculations. Would it be better to sell your car and just use a cab service if you need to go somewhere public transportation won't take you? Cut back on expensive entertainment. Rent a movie rather than go out to the cinema. Cut back on all those cable channels. And stop giving charitable donations or gifts.

There's one thing you shouldn't scrimp on, though: health coverage for you and your family. It can be expensive, but it's essential: One uninsured fractured leg could use up your entire savings and put you back to square one. See if you can continue on your old firm's coverage for a year. The cost of finding a health plan without the backing of a company actually persuades some people to begin part-time so they can keep their benefits. Find out whether any associations that deal with your field offer health plans.

Now let's go back and examine the options you have for covering these monthly expenditures. Can you live on one income? It helps to have someone else in your household earning money. By that we mean a spouse or a significant other who is earning a regular, dependable wage, not your son and his paper route. If, with a little scrimping and saving, your partner can provide enough for your family to live on, then you'll be able to start up a lot quicker.

Can you live off your savings for about eight to ten months? You're in a great position financially if you can answer "yes" to this question. Even so, you should still put yourself on an austerity budget. After all, the less money you use on yourself, the more money you have available to put towards your business. If your spouse isn't working, you may want to talk about him or her taking a part-time job—the extra cash can only be useful. The danger, if you choose to go by this method, is that you may be tempted to start taking money back from the business before it's ready to give anything. It's easier to maintain a strict split between your living costs and your business expenses when there is a different source of income for each one.

Can you start up part-time? If you're the only money-maker in the family, and you don't have a great deal of savings, this is often the alternative of choice. Many traditional business advisers like to come out against this route, however. They say things like, "Never start a business part-time ... It's halfhearted ... You need to make a commitment." We disagree. As a 21st Century entrepreneur, your commitment is assured, as is your grasp of the business climate and the market. So we feel the choice of starting up full-time or part-time is entirely up to you. It all depends on how much of a risk you're willing, or able, to take. Trust your own judgment.

The final option, of course, is paying yourself a sufficient salary right from the start. This may turn out to be wildly optimistic, but we'll explore it further when we go into the financial planning.

At *RIFP* we decided that Melissa would keep her day job and Ben would work full-time on the newsletter. That way we managed to keep our medical benefits and assure ourselves of some income. We filled out the list of expenses, and it looked like this:

Mortgage or rent payment	$1,580
Debt service	$0
Tax payment	$100
Insurance	$8
Utilities	$75
Telephone	$85
Household maintenance	$140
Nonreimbursable medical	$40
Auto	$0
Food	$300
Entertainment	$0
Total monthly expenses	$2,328

That came to a yearly outlay of $27,936. We added our onetime yearly expenses and came up with a total of $28,100 per year or $2,340 per month. This was more than Melissa earned at the time, so we knew we had to cut back. The largest monthly expense, our mortgage and co-op maintenance, was a constant, and we knew the maintenance would probably go up at some point. We didn't have any outstanding debts on cars or furniture, so we were ahead there. Our tax estimate was based on what we had paid the prior year. The next year's taxes might be different, but since the bill had never been larger than $1,500, we thought we'd probably be okay. Cable TV came under the heading of utilities, and we decided that was one luxury we could cut out. We also pledged to write people letters rather than call them—especially our relatives in Europe. That would cut down our telephone bills. Household maintenance was a catchall category for everything from cleaning supplies and light bulbs to bookcases and the odd things we tended to bring home. That was definitely an area ready for pruning. The medical expenses we budgeted were merely the cost of keeping Ben on Melissa's health plan. If something went wrong, we could expect larger bills, but not as large as they'd be if we had no insurance. There was no way to lower that expense. We didn't have a car, so that saved us a lot of money. Food was one place we could actually save money. We stopped eating out and ordering food in. Best of all, we joined a local food cooperative where, in return for putting in three hours of work a month, we could buy food in bulk and at cost. It meant we had to plan our menus ahead and persuade a friend to drive us there every couple of weeks, but it did cut our food bills drastically. Here's how the list looked after we cut it down:

Mortgage or rent payment	$1,580
Debt service	$0
Tax payment	$100
Insurance	$8
Utilities	$45
Telephone	$60
Household maintenance	$70
Nonreimbursable medical	$40
Auto	$0
Food	$120
Entertainment	$0
Total monthly expenses	$2,023

That came to a grand total of $24,276 per year. After adding a couple of hundred dollars for annual bills, we gave ourselves a yearly budget of $24,500 or about $2,040 a month. If we kept to that amount, we would be able to save $4,000 a year that we could put towards the newsletter.

YOUR START-UP COSTS

Now you've worked out how much money you'll need to live on while your business becomes profitable. Before you can work out how long that will take, you must calculate one last lump sum—the amount of money you'll have to spend before you can open for business. This section of the chapter will calculate everything you'll need in order to get you to opening day.

DEPOSITS

If you're renting a space, you're going to need deposits for the telephone, utility, and insurance companies, not to mention your landlord. If you're working from home, you'll only need to deal with the phone company.

OFFICE EQUIPMENT

Your needs will be very particular, so we're only going to discuss equipment briefly. The first thing you'll want to sort out is your telephone. You can't afford to allow customers to hear a busy signal, so you'll either need to get Call Waiting or, if you can afford it, two lines. Business rates are expensive (about three times more than residential rates), and it's illegal to use a residential telephone line for business.

You'll also need a decent telephone (rather than the one you got free with a subscription to *Time*). You want to buy a solid-looking telephone, one that could survive a shower of coffee or a fall to the floor. If you have two lines, you'll need to be able to put someone on hold. If you do a lot of calling, you might want speed dialing. Think about whether customers are going to be visiting your office. If they are, get an extension so that they don't need to sit at your desk (and read your notes or spot the unflattering caricatures you drew). Don't bother paying for conference call capability unless you use it twice a week. Forget call forwarding: You can keep in touch by calling your answering machine from telephone booths.

While we're talking about telephones, there are two other related products you'll need: a telephone answering machine and, most likely, a fax machine. You're going to need a good answering machine. Whether or not you have two lines now, buy it with two-line capacity just in case. Make sure you can call in to it and get your messages easily. A fax machine may be crucial to your business. Decide what you're going to use it for and then buy the model that best fits your needs. Speed isn't going to be the priority here. What you want is a document feeder and a built-in page cutter. Memory is useful if you're going to be sending documents to different time zones. The cost of plain-paper fax machines is coming down all the time. They cost a little more than fax-paper machines, but the documents don't fade and they're easier to file and copy.

If your entire business is going to be conducted with handshakes and organized on the backs of envelopes, then you can do without a computer. Otherwise you should buy one. A computer can't magically solve problems for you, but it can take a lot of the drudge work out of keeping financial records and writing letters. Think hard and long about which one to buy. Oddly, the first thing you should decide on is the software you want, rather than the actual computer. Try to buy the most basic version you can. You'll probably want something that can do word processing, spreadsheets, and perhaps simple data bases. There are a number of simple programs out there that combine all three of these. Microsoft Works is very popular. Beware; the sales staff in a computer store will always try to convince you to buy a more sophisticated version than you'll actually need. It's not simply that they're trying to get more money out of you. They're also suffering from a side effect of being computer geeks. Just as bikers live vicariously through one another's bikes, so computerphiles love to think about people using the latest program update. They genuinely feel they've helped spread the cause of computers if they convince you that you need a thesaurus and alphabetical "columnizing." Of course, your business may have special needs, in which case you should listen cautiously to the advice of the sales staff and consult one of the sources we recommend at the end of the chapter for the appropriate information.

Once you've picked a program you think will work, you need to decide on the computer. Your first big choice is whether you are going to get a Macintosh or a copy—or clone, as it's called in the computer business—of an IBM. (No one in his right mind would pay the high price of a genuine IBM, and most of the clones are just as good as the originals, if not better.) If your software is only made for Macs or clones, then the decision is made for you. If not, then you should bear in mind the following: It used to be that Macintosh computers were considered hideously expensive but great to work with, whereas IBM clones were hard to work with, but cheap. It's not that simple anymore since Apple reduced the price of its Macs. The bottom-line Macs are now within most people's reach. However, for the same money you can probably get more computer memory and speed from the IBM clone. The price of computers has been falling rapidly for the last decade or so. Today, for the same money, you can buy twice the computer you could five years ago.

You might also want to consider whether you want a laptop computer or a standard desktop one. There's no appreciable difference between the memory or speed of a desktop and a laptop. The advantage of a laptop is that you can take it off your desk if you need the space and bring it with you if you travel. The disadvantages are that the screens can sometimes be difficult to read and the keyboards can be smaller. If you need to do graphics, you'll probably want the size and clarity of a desktop screen.

Next you need to choose a printer. There are three basic options here: laser, dot matrix, and bubble jet. Laser printers give the clearest print and are almost silent. However, despite some price cutting, they're still very expensive. Dot matrix printers are the cheapest and noisiest, but they've become more sophisticated and can produce text that looks almost as good as that from a laser printer or typewriter. Bubble jets never really caught on because of some early problems with the ink smudging. These problems have been sorted out, and many people swear by them. You'll need to see each kind in action before you choose.

Before you buy anything to do with the computer, think carefully about why you're buying it. Are you succumbing to hard drive and option envy? Have you been infected with the most deadly computer virus, the foolish notion that "more is better"? If you're only going to use the computer to write letters, you could get away with a whole package—software, computer, and printer—for under one thousand dollars.

There may be other office equipment peculiar to your business that you need in your office—medical or dental equipment, for example. Our best advice is to consider leasing it. Leasing spreads the cost out, gives you the option of upgrades, and also frees you from the worry of paying for repairs.

Unless you spend more than an hour a week at the copy shop,

don't bother buying your own copy machine. There's a good reason everyone in those shops is always in a foul mood: Copy machines break down continuously, smell, and are noisy. And, as we advised in the last chapter, buy secondhand filing cabinets and a good chair.

STATIONERY

Go to a professional printer and get yourself some simple, classy business cards: black on white, with your logo if you have one, and your name. Think carefully before choosing a fancy typeface; you probably want to come across as professional rather than zany. Do the same with some letterhead paper and envelopes, but do yourself a favor and don't order too much: Should you go under, there's nothing sadder than piles of unused stationery. If you're a success, you can always order some more. Don't think that a large supply of stationery or a closet full of supplies signifies that you're a "real" business.

TRANSPORTATION

You may need transportation for your service business. If this means public transportation, find out whether there are any discount tickets. If you need a van or a car, again, consider leasing, at least until after the first year. You'll want to talk the whole thing over with your insurance agent.

SIGNS

The car or van you use for business is essentially a large, four-wheeled, 35-mpg business card. So, even if it's old, keep it clean inside and out, and make sure your company's name is printed neatly on the side. Avoid those free yellow pages stickers that come with your name on them, unless you're a plumber. Get some decent, classy signs for your office. If you use a poster painter to advertise from your office windows, make sure he or she knows the rudiments of grammar and spelling.

PROFESSIONAL FEES

We've saved the worst for last. If you don't consult these professionals, you'll be out of business within six months. The good news is that, although their fees will hurt you as you go through the year, for the start-up process, the fees are negligible. The 21st Century entrepreneur is supposed to be an all-around competent person, but no one expects you to know the intimate details of tax or real estate law. There are three professionals who will be invaluable to you and your company. In order of importance, they are: your accountant, your lawyer, and your insurance broker.

You should find them through personal recommendation from people who are in similar businesses to yours. Schedule a meeting with each professional and ask some pertinent questions about their experience with businesses like yours. Don't be afraid to ask them "why?" all the time. After all, they're the experts. Ask why they do things in a certain way. Why you must go through whatever arcane procedures they want you to go through. By the time you've compared a few of these professionals you'll be pretty clear about who you want to have working for you. Always remember that's the way the relationship works: They work for you. All of these professionals should be happy to take the time to explain whatever it is they are doing. You should be able to learn from them; not in order to supplant them, but to add to your knowledge of what is happening to your business. Don't be afraid to ask them how much they charge. If the fee seems high, ask why it's two hundred dollars rather than asking why it's so high. Ask to be sent weekly bills so you can keep track of what's going on. Ask whether you can work out a payment plan that might spread some of the initial fee over the first few months.

YOUR ACCOUNTANT

Your accountant should be a business-oriented CPA, not a tax preparer or your brother-in-law who "knows about these things." You need someone who is conscientious about keeping up with the latest tax laws. You can pretty much trust CPAs since they'll jeopardize their license if they aren't professional. Your CPA should have some experience in helping to start up small businesses. But it's all right if he's young. That could mean he's willing to grow with your company and be willing to charge less. There will be an initial charge as he sorts out your business, and then you'll be charged for individual services during the year. He'll probably charge between fifty and two hundred dollars an hour. You'll find his advice invaluable when calculating your start-up costs and even more valuable when working out your break-even point, which you'll learn about in the next chapter. He'll also help you work out the legal structure of your business. You can either be a sole proprietor, a partnership, or a corporation. Let's digress from the discussion of professionals for a few paragraphs to briefly touch on this structure topic.

THE STRUCTURE OF YOUR BUSINESS

A *sole proprietorship* means things are kept simple. You run the business and you own the business. You save on lawyer and accountant bills. Whatever money the business makes is your money, you get to keep it. You are flexible and can make the decisions and take the responsibility for your actions. On the other hand, if you get into debt and creditors come a-knocking, all your assets are fair game for them, including your survival money, house, car, and firstborn. It's also more of a risk for your family: If you go under because of sickness, so does your business. Finally, it's harder to get financing than if you were in a partnership or a corporation.

A *partnership* is a little more complicated. You'll need a lawyer to sort out who does what, and how much they get paid for it. You'll need to discuss, for example: how long the partnership will run; how you'll divide the profits and losses; what you'll do if one of you dies; what you'll do if you argue; and what's known as the *character of partners*. This means whether you'll be equal partners and whether you'll both be involved in the running of the business, or whether your partner will be silent.

There are advantages to being a partnership rather than a sole proprietorship. For a start, you have access to someone else's experience, ideas, and, most of all, bank balance. Your partner can balance your skills and weaknesses: If you work well with calculators and she works well with people, then you may do well. Like a sole proprietorship, it's comparatively easy to set up a partnership, and any money you make comes directly to you and your partner. Naturally, there are a number of disadvantages. While you're more flexible than a corporation, you're less able to adapt than a sole proprietorship. Also, at least one of you in the partnership has to have unlimited liability, just like a sole proprietorship. You're also dependent on the other person. (See Chapter Eleven for more thoughts about choosing a partner.) Your combined capital will be larger than a sole proprietorship's (we hope), but you'll still find long-term financing difficult.

Corporations are quite complex, so this is just a quick overview. Corporations give your business more cachet and your family more protection, but they can be unwieldy to run. Corporations can either be C corporations or, if there are thirty-five or fewer shareholders, it can be subchapter S. The difference lies in the types of stock and how profits are taxed. Subchapter S corporations are not taxed as heavily as C corporations.

The major advantage to incorporating is that your liability is limited to the capital put in. You can also sell your shares easily. If someone falls ill or dies, the corporation can still continue. It's also easier to get financing: You can issue long-term stock and bonds to build up capital. The major disadvantage is the cost of setting up as a corporation, although people have been known to do it without lawyers and accountants. You'll also find yourself having to pay attention to hundreds of state and federal laws. You'll need to make all sorts of reports to the city, state, and federal government.

One choice many entrepreneurs make is to begin as a sole proprietorship and go on to form a corporation when the business is under way. These are just a few of the advantages and disadvantages to each kind of legal structure. Your accountant can take you through the choices more thoroughly and help you choose which will be best for you. Let's get back to the members of your professional team.

Your Attorney

Your attorney should be a generalist, someone with a broad range of experience. Rely on him or her to call in specialists when needed. Your lawyer should be more experienced than your CPA. The increased experience will benefit you because you can learn from other people's mistakes, and the contacts he has made will be useful: You're hiring his Rolodex as well as his skill. Look for a lawyer who works alone, or in a small firm, rather than in a large partnership. Make sure he charges by the hour. Try to get an estimate for how much you'll be paying him to help you start the business. The fees will probably be somewhere between $150 and $200 an hour. (Whenever we think about this, we seriously consider putting each other through law school.)

Your Insurance Broker

An insurance broker is also a crucial member of your team. Your surprise at this statement will vanish once you start calculating how much all your coverages will cost you. Your broker should be a member of a large firm of business-oriented insurance brokers. You want to beware of fly-by-night operators who promise experience and say they're willing to search for the best rates but really only offer you the policies of one company. A good insurance broker will be willing to help you collect money owed to you, as well as set you up with the policy. Only your broker can assess exactly what kind of coverage you'll need, but you'll probably have to consider at least some of the following: theft, visitor and legal liability, fire, business interruption (to tide you over after a disaster), automobile insurance, and—depending on whether or not you have employees—worker's compensation. Don't cut costs by scrimping on your insurance. A good broker won't let you, but don't be tempted. Ed Alleva, Jr., says that when explaining the high cost of a policy, his father always used to say, "I'd rather keep you as a friend, and lose you as a client," meaning that, as an honest man, he couldn't sell someone a policy that didn't adequately cover his or her needs. You're taking enough of a risk as it is without wondering what would happen if something went terribly wrong. The good news is, there are no fees: The broker is given a commission for selling you the policy.

RIFP'S START-UP COSTS

At *RIFP* we went through this whole process. We talked with Elysa Lazar, publisher of *S&B Reports,* and Stuart Bauman of Bauman & Krasnoff, a CPA firm in New York City, to arrive at some of our initial figures. In retrospect, we realize we had it easy in some ways, particularly because we could live on only one salary and one of us could work at home. On the other hand, we were working in a major metropolitan area, so prices are high. What follows is a record of everything we actually spent. This will give you an idea of what your start-up costs might be. Before we went out and spent anything, we estimated what it would cost and made sure we had enough in our savings.

OFFICE EQUIPMENT

We needed to put in a new telephone line, and pay for touch-tone service. We also had to buy a new telephone and an answering machine that makes it sound as though it's us, and not the iguanas, answering the phone.

We had always used a word-processing program called Xywrite, simply because many of the magazines we had written for used it. Its great advantage is that it translates easily into the language that typesetters use. The disadvantage is that it's complicated to learn, but we overcame that five years ago. Recently Xywrite came out with an update that combined the speed of its original program with a desktop package. It's called Xywrite IV, and after testing it, we decided that was what we wanted to use. We chose a software package called Quicken to keep track of our finances. It came to us recommended by a friend and had everything we needed at a good price.

Xywrite only works on IBM-compatible machines, so we had to get one of those. We needed a computer that could handle our financial info, as well as our typing and our simple graphic needs. We chose a midrange IBM clone, one with a 286 processor and forty megabytes of memory. There were and are more sophisticated (and more expensive) computers out there, but this did what we needed. We splurged and bought a laser printer. That was because we wanted everything to look professional, especially since we were working from home.

We picked up a couple of two-drawer filing cabinets from a tag sale. At the local lumber store we bought a piece of wood and put it on top of them to make a large desk. We invested in two beautiful faded orange chairs from a secondhand office furniture store.

IBM AT clone, monochrome monitor, and mouse	$1,200
New telephone	$90
New telephone line installed	$300
New answering machine	$75
Xywrite IV upgrade	$99
Financial software	$50
Laser printer	$1,100
Filing cabinets (2 @ $50)	$100
Wood	$26
Chairs (2 @ $50)	$100
Total	$3,140

STATIONERY

We went to our local print shop and got some business cards printed. We liked the results, so we ordered some letterhead paper and envelopes.

1,000 business cards	$30
100 sheets of letterhead paper	$26
100 envelopes	$30
Total	$86

SIGNS

We weren't going to announce to our neighbors what we were doing, so we didn't need any signs.

TRANSPORTATION

We didn't need any transportation, except to and from the printer with the finished newsletter.

DEPOSITS

The phone company needed a three-hundred-dollar deposit, which was returned after a year of timely payments (with a massive 6 percent interest added on).

PROFESSIONAL FEES

As it happened, the accountants we went to for our taxes every year actually spend most of their time working with small businesses, so we decided to stick with them. They were able to give us a good estimate about how much it would cost us to have them sit down and work out all the finances—one hundred dollars.

The lawyer who handled the purchase of our apartment recommended a generalist he knows who has had experience with small businesses. After a positive meeting with this new lawyer, we decided to use him. He advised us that, as we were setting up business as a sole proprietorship, we really didn't need his help. We only had to file one form down at city hall, a DBA (doing business as). This cost us eighty-five dollars and meant the business was legally called Raising Iguanas for Fun and Profit. We also had to apply for an EIN (employer identification number), basically a Social Security number for the company. We thanked our lawyer and told him we'd be back to seek his advice in the future.

The same lawyer recommended our insurance broker. We checked with a couple of other lawyer friends, and they knew of her and hadn't heard anything negative, so we went to talk. She seemed professional, her prices were competitive compared with three other brokers we called up, and so we hired her. And, of course, there were no fees for her services. Our total start-up costs for professionals was $185.

Here's a breakdown of what we needed to get the business off the ground:

Office equipment	$3,140
Stationery	$86
Deposits	$300
Professional fees	$185
Total start-up costs	$3,711

Bear in mind that had we been starting a different business or not working from home, our deposits and professional fees might have been much higher. Our savings covered this amount comfortably, so we were able to move on to the next step.

We didn't need to add in any survival money because we were going to try and survive on Melissa's wages. By going through all these figures, we knew how much money it would take to get to opening day. If you go through the same process, you'll have a good idea of how much money you'll need to keep yourself in clothes and food before your business can actually support you.

In the next chapter you're going to estimate how much money it will cost you to keep your business going until it begins to make a profit. This money is called *working capital*. We'll also show you how to estimate how long it will take you to break even, and how much you can charge for your service.

For more information on the topics covered in Chapter Nine, take a look at the following books:

- *Incorporating a Small Business,* by Alan J. Parker (PLI, 1987)
- *Incorporating Your Talents: A Guide To the One-Person Corporation, or How to Lead a Sheltered Life,* by Robert A. Esperti and Renno L. Peterson (McGraw, 1984)
- *Starting a Business of Your Own—With ''No'' Money,* by David F. Cox (Empire, 1990)
- *Starting on a Shoestring: Building a Business Without a Bankroll,* by Arnold S. Goldstein (Wiley, 1991)
- *Starting Shoestring Businesses: Steady Profits on a Full-Time or Part-Time Basis* (Gordon, 1992)

⟷ 10 ⟷
WASHING WINDOWS

Calculating Fees and Working Capital Needs

In this chapter we're going to finish explaining the financial preparations for setting up your business. We've already dealt with start-up costs—how much it will take to get to opening day. Now we're going to examine pricing and working capital—how much money your company will need to stay in business until it begins to make a profit. Another way to think of your working capital is as a temporary fund for your company. In the last chapter we figured out how much money you'd need to keep yourself in food and clothes. The working capital is the money that's supposed to tide your business over until it makes enough to cover its own monthly and yearly costs. Basically you're in a race to become profitable before this fund dries up. Let's take you through the process.

Each month you'll have costs you must meet. We'll talk about these in more detail later, but for now think of them as things like rent and phone bills. At the start, because your company isn't bringing in any money, you'll need to meet the costs by using a temporary fund—your working capital. Because you essentially owe money at the end of every month and need to meet the bills with your working capital, your cash flow is considered "negative." As time goes on, your revenue will increase, and because of this, you'll need to use less and less of your working capital to meet the costs. Your working capital will still shrink, but less rapidly than before. Eventually, one month, your business will bring in the same amount of money as it costs to keep it going. Your cash flow is now "neutral" and you have broken even. It's a good place to be, but you're not out of the woods yet. As soon as you start making more money than you spend every month, your cash flow becomes "positive."

Let's go through the same process with a simple example of a window-washing business. Tom Morris quit his job as a sales clerk and decided to set up business as a window washer. He had washed windows before, and, in fact, he thought he was pretty good at it. However, it had never been his sole source of income. He had enough money saved for his family to live on for eight months. His start-up costs included a pickup truck and a large, top-quality aluminum ladder. To keep his business functioning he needed sufficient working capital to pay for buckets, soap, and parking, and gas for his truck.

To begin with, things didn't go exactly as he planned. He didn't get the amount of business he thought he would, and he even had a little difficulty learning more refined techniques of wiping and washing. Eventually, after a few months of hard work, he found that business was picking up and he was earning more every month. Or, to put it another way, he was losing less every month. Eight months later, he sat down and added up his earnings and expenses for the past four weeks: Surprise! He'd earned as much as he spent. Morris had broken even, and even though he wasn't rolling in cash, he was much better off than when he'd started. He had acquired a skill, regular customers, and a reputation as an excellent window washer.

This chapter will tell you how to calculate your working capital. Before you can do that, however, you have to work out how much you should charge for your service. Why? Because before you can work out how much money you're going to need as working capital, you have to estimate how much you'll earn. And, of course, that is tied in with how much you'll charge. We'll discuss how to tell when you've reached the break-even point. Then we'll take you through what we did for our newsletter, *RIFP,* and how we figured out our working capital and how much a subscription would cost.

CALCULATING YOUR WORKING CAPITAL

We'll help you get started in this calculation, but be aware that at some point you'll need to sit down with your accountant to work out the final details. You will have two kinds of costs that drain your working capital: *variable costs* and *fixed costs*.

Variable costs change with your business flow. The more business you get, the higher the total cost of your supplies. You can think of it as the cost of your sales. For Tom Morris, soap is a variable cost. The more he washes, the more he has to spend on soap. For our newsletter, postage will be a variable cost. If our number of subscribers increases, then we'll need to spend more on postage. The wages and benefits you pay employees are considered variable costs since, by hiring, promoting, or firing, the numbers can change.

Fixed costs, as you might expect, are those that don't change. For the window washer, the monthly cost of a parking space in the center of town would be a fixed cost. For our newsletter, fixed costs include paying the accountant and the credit card fees, as well as the cost of advertising and promotions we do on an unchanging, regular basis. Rent, transportation, cleaning, and maintenance are some of the fixed costs you may incur.

Your salary is a fixed cost. If you're the only working member of your family, you need to pay yourself enough to live on. Make it realistic, but make it cast iron. Don't buy yourself a new television until you've broken even for three or four months.

At this point it's a good idea to go back to some of the businesses you talked to when you were choosing your idea. Ask them what their fixed costs are. Utility companies can give you a good estimate of what those bills will be like. Trade associations can also help you figure out monthly costs.

Your hardworking accountant will figure out your taxes. Taxes will take a bite out of the money you end up with, but we're going to leave them out of the calculations because each person will have a different level of taxation. Here's a brief explanation. If you are running a sole proprietorship or a partnership, you'll be taxed as an individual. If you are running a corporation, the tax rate will vary, but can go as high as 50 percent. And then your salary will be taxed. Taxes are complicated and expensive: They can include a commercial-rent tax, some of your landlord's tax, federal, state, local, and (if you're not a corporation) even an unincorporated-business tax. This in addition to Social Security contributions for any employees you might have. Your accountant is clearly going to play a key part in all of this figuring. Over the year, he or she will charge you somewhere between one thousand and three thousand dollars. Pay the bill graciously. This whole process of calculating your working capital sounds hideously complicated. But take it one step at a time, and eventually you'll come up with a final figure.

As you read through the chapter, the following worksheet will help you keep track of how far you've come. We've included another copy of this worksheet in Appendix C.

Task	Date Begun	Date Completed
(1) Estimate monthly fixed costs: rent, salary, utilities, advertising, etc.	_____	_____
(2) Estimate monthly variable costs: supplies, others' salaries, etc.	_____	_____
(3) Estimate your fees according to your billable hours per week.	_____	_____
(4) Work out when the fees will allow you to break even.	_____	_____
(5) Calculate working capital—i.e., the money needed to keep your business afloat until you've broken even.	_____	_____

RIFP WORKING CAPITAL

At *RIFP* we estimated our fixed and variable costs. To do this we talked to people who ran newsletters and to our team of professionals. Here is what we came up with. Of course, at the time it was impossible to pin down the numbers precisely, so remember that these were estimates and were subject to lots of revision. We first looked at our fixed annual costs:

RIFP FIXED ANNUAL COSTS

Accountant	$2,000
Lawyer	$750
Insurance for apartment	$195
Advertising and promotions	$200
Credit card fees	$100
Telephone service ($34 × 12 months)	$408
Telephone use ($200 × 12 months)	$2,400
Membership in a couple of reptile associations	$80
Total fixed annual costs	$3,733
Total fixed monthly costs ($3,733 ÷ 12 months)	$311

Our variable costs would depend on how much business we were doing. We thought our two variable costs would be postage and printing. Naturally, the more subscriptions we sold, the more we'd have to pay in postage. Printing was different: As it turned out, the printer wouldn't print fewer than one thousand copies. We don't expect to be selling that many copies to begin with, so, in effect, the printing is a fixed cost. We will list it under a variable cost since, in the future, it may vary more than it does now.

The next job was to work out how much we were going to charge for our service. Let's take a look at how to come up with those numbers.

HOW MUCH TO CHARGE FOR YOUR SERVICE: THE BIG QUESTION

It used to be that everyone, the window washer included, had to be aware of, and charge, the going rate. But as a 21st Century entrepreneur, you should find out what the going rate is so you can ignore it. You probably asked about fees when you were researching your ideas, so look back at your notes. The figures your rivals gave you are just rough guidelines. You'll be able to charge up to a third more because your company will be unique. Not only will it be geared toward the 21st Century, it'll be offering real value for money, not just lip service. An important thing to realize about pricing services is that people often believe that the more they pay for a service, the better it is. Charge more, look and act successful, and you'll make more money.

Lewis Lipnick, owner of Your Silent Partner, was lucky enough to find someone early on to give him pricing advice. "I used to charge a flat fee for a consultation and for installation. But I knew I was spending too much time on each job, and, in fact, I was losing money. One of my clients kindly told me I was making a mistake. She told me I was doing something unique, and that I was doing it well. She said I could charge a lot more for it. To begin with, I thought people would laugh when I told them the fee, or that they wouldn't take the service. But they didn't, and they did, and now I charge $150 an hour or $1,500 a day."

There's no easy way to figure out exactly what you should charge. It's a matter of juggling and balancing. We'll show you how we found out how much we wanted to charge for our newsletter in a moment. You must go through the same imprecise process for yourself. You'll need to ask yourself lots of questions like "If I charge this much and get this much work, will I be better off than if I charged 20 percent more and worked fewer hours?" If you're starting a service that has some sort of product attached to it, then you must decide how many of these products you can sell, as in the case of our newsletter. Once again, find out from competitors how many products they sell. Get friends and relatives to ask your rivals questions. Finding out the circulation of a news-paper or magazine is easy: You just call and pretend you want to advertise. For other companies, pretend you're interested in investing . . . or just ask them the information you want point-blank. If you're not a direct rival or are in a different part of the country, they may just tell you.

If you plan to bill people for the hours you work for them, like a lawyer, then calculate how many billable hours a day you can actually work. The billable hour is your product. Tom Morris, the window cleaner, can only work during daylight. But that doesn't give him an eight-hour workday: He has to factor in the time it takes to travel around at work, his lunch break, and the time needed to do his accounts, as well as time for setting up advertising and finding new clients. Once you know roughly how many bill-able hours or products you could sell, you should estimate how many you actually will sell. There are two key points here: Re-member to set your fee higher than your initial impulse, and also underestimate how much business you'll do. The same optimism that led you to start your business may also lead you to mistakenly believe your business will break even faster than it actually will. Your confidence has to be tempered by common sense.

RIFP PRICING

Now that you know how to set your fees, have a look at the process in practice. We tried all sorts of different prices before we decided on the cost of a subscription to our iguana newsletter. Deciding was a matter of finding the right balance between num-ber of subscribers and price. If you need to make thirty thousand dollars, then you can find one person to pay thirty thousand dol-lars, or you can find thirty thousand people to pay a dollar each. The key is balancing subscribers and price.

What follows are just four examples of the calculations we made to come up with a subscription price. In order to proceed, we assumed that postage would remain at twenty-nine cents. We wanted to send out fifty promotional mailings every month, so the cost of this extra fifty ($50 $\times$ .29 = $14.50) is added to the postage. As we said, our variable costs actually remain fairly static because the printer won't print fewer than one thousand newsletters, for which he charges $144. You'll notice that we didn't plan on drawing any wages. This was because we calculated that we could survive on Melissa's wages from her full-time job. We were also being ambitious in our estimates, assuming that we could sell enough subscriptions to break even within a year. For most businesses it takes between eight months and fourteen months before that happens. Each of the first three examples varied the conditions for one month; the final example looked at what would happen after a year. Any number that's in parentheses means it's negative, or a deficit.

EXAMPLE 1

This example calculated the price we'd need to charge in order to break even. We assumed we could sell thirteen subscriptions a month, for a year, giving us a total of 156 subscriptions.

Price of one subscription:	$30	$40	$50	$100
Revenue (price × 13 subscriptions):	$390	$520	$650	$1,300
Less fixed costs:	$311	$311	$311	$311
Less variable costs:				
Printing:	$144	$144	$144	$144
Postage:	$19	$19	$19	$19
Loss:	($84)	$0	$0	$0
Net profit before tax:	$0	$46	$176	$826

In other words, if we found thirteen subscribers and charged them $40 for twelve issues of the newsletter, we'd be able to break even that month. If we could keep that up for the whole year and we managed to find 156 subscribers, we'd be running a profitable business. There wouldn't be a lot of profit ($46 × 12 = $552), and we'd need to make it stretch a long way to cover our living expenses. It would, however, bode well for the business, as long as we continued to attract subscribers.

EXAMPLE 2

What would happen if the number of subscribers rose or fell from thirteen? To answer this question, we kept the cost of a subscription at $50 and changed the number of subscribers. You'll notice the cost of the postage went up because of the increase in subscribers.

Subscriptions sold at $50:	8	15	18	22
Revenue:	$400	$750	$900	$1,100
Less fixed costs:	$311	$311	$311	$311
Less variable costs:				
Printing:	$144	$144	$144	$144
Postage:	$17	$19	$20	$21
Loss:	($72)	$0	$0	$0
Net profit before tax:	$0	$276	$425	$624

Remarkably, a difference of only three subscribers made a big difference in the profits. We learned that our profits would increase a lot faster than our variable costs. Our variable costs increased by only $4 between columns 1 and 4, whereas our profits grew from less than zero to $624. We also learned, however, that we were really going to need to watch our subscription base carefully—it represented a thin line between life and debt.

EXAMPLE 3

In the first example we saw the profit that could be made by charging $50 or $100 for the newsletter. We thought that $100 was on the high end of what we could charge for twelve issues of *RIFP*. But we remembered that service business entrepreneurs tend to undercharge for their services. This example shows what happened when we tried different prices for the newsletter and still sold thirteen subscriptions a month.

Cost of one subscription:	$75	$150	$200
Revenue for one month:	$975	$1,950	$2,600
Less fixed costs:	$311	$311	$311

Less variable costs:			
Printing:	$144	$144	$144
Postage:	$19	$19	$19
Net profit before tax:	$501	$1,476	$2,126

In our previous example, fifteen subscribers buying subscriptions costing $50 gave us $276 profit. Here we saw that fewer subscribers, thirteen, paying $75 made us almost twice as much money—$501. We were more worried about finding enough people to subscribe than whether or not they could afford the newsletter since our market research had shown that iguana owners have a lot of money to spend on leisure. From this we concluded that it would probably be easier to sell a few people an expensive service rather than many people a cheap one (see Chapter Thirteen).

EXAMPLE 4

After working through all these examples, we sat down and made some decisions about *RIFP*. We were going to make the cost of a subscription to the newsletter seventy-five dollars and aim to sell 156 subscriptions in the first year. If that happened, we would have broken even, made a good profit, and wouldn't actually need any working capital to cover the deficiency. But then we examined what would happen if we didn't get 156 subscribers in a year.

Subscriptions sold at $75 during year:	50	80	100
Revenue:	$3,750	$6,000	$7,500
Less fixed costs ($311 × 12):	$3,722	$3,722	$3,732
Less variable costs:			
Printing:	$1,728	$1,728	$1,728
Postage (average):	$188	$197	$201
Loss:	($1,888)	$0	$0
Net profit before tax:	$0	$353	$1,839

In order to break even, we needed to make sure that we sold eighty subscriptions in the first year. That was about seven subscribers a month. (In Chapter Fifteen we'll show you how to keep track of whether or not you're meeting your needs and are on target for making a profit.) We aimed at breaking even within a year. As we said, that was ambitious. If you go through the same process and find that you'll owe money at the end of the year, you're in the same boat as we would be in column 1 of example 4: You would have a working capital deficit.

There are ways to rectify this. You could raise your prices or find a larger market and so increase your customers. But be realistic. Remember that entrepreneurs frequently think they'll attract more clients than they actually do. The other, more practical solution is to give your business longer than a year to break even. You can plan ahead for the working capital deficiency and put the money aside before you open for business. As we said at the beginning, it's a temporary fund for your business to live off until it can fend for itself. You should add it to your start-up costs in order to get the total amount of money it will cost to start your business.

Having read the last two chapters, you should be confident about the financial planning that should go into starting your business. You know what starting your business is going to cost and how much you're going to charge for your services. You may even feel like taking off in your pickup truck and setting yourself up as a window cleaner. The key is to find some cold, hard numbers and start experimenting with them.

From now on we're dealing with facts. You're now prepared to talk about this business as a real business. You probably don't have the actual money yet, but at least you know exactly what you need. The next chapter will tell you where to find it.

For more information on the topics covered in Chapter Ten, take a look at the following book:

- *Time Is Money: Selling Your Professional Services,* by Richard Creedy (New American Library, 1980)

11

THE RECESSION REBELLION

How Will You Find Your Seed Money?

Your start-up costs plus your working capital is the amount of seed money you need. The last two chapters showed you how to calculate how much this will be. This chapter will tell you where to find it. The recession of the early 1990s had an unpleasant effect on our pocketbooks, but it did teach Americans to be wary about banks. This is something of a rebellion in our way of thinking. Not as strong as a revolution, but definitely a shift in the way we think about finance.

Our old illusions have been shattered. Nothing much has changed yet, but we no longer think that banks are benign institutions, doing us a favor by letting us put our hard-earned money in their coffers. Banks are beginning to think that they should be looking after their customers. A lot of banks made lousy real estate deals in the eighties and haven't been making the money they hoped to. They are coming to terms with the fact that they should remember to cater to the consistent small-time investor and depositor rather than always going for the big deal.

Banks are not yet at the stage where they are willing to lend small businesses money for starting up. That's why we advised you not to go to the trouble of writing a formal business plan—it's just not worth the effort. Soon, perhaps, bank officers will be given the opportunity to take small risks and will lend entrepreneurs the measly six thousand dollars they are asking for. Right now consider it the banks' loss. You'll be continuing the rebellion by looking for alternative sources of finance. In two years, when you come to expand your business, you can then go to a bank and see what it has to offer you.

We're going to briefly run through some of the old ways of financing, just in case you see an opening somewhere and want to take advantage of it, but we're going to concentrate mostly on some of the new ways you can find money.

In order to raise money, one thing is paramount. You need to have your own money invested. If you aren't risking your life savings (except, of course, for the survival money you budgeted in Chapter Nine), then no one is going to take you seriously. After all, why should they risk their money when you aren't risking yours?

THE OLD WAYS OF FINANCING A START-UP BUSINESS

PARTNERSHIPS

There are two kinds of partnerships—financial and strategic. Strategic partnerships—or alliances, as they're often called—are a key characteristic of 21st Century service businesses. They allow small businesses to expand and contract rapidly by joining with other companies for specific projects for which services are pooled and bartered. We'll talk more about these later.

This section deals with financial partnerships. These were once a good way to get start-up money. The theory was that two, or even three, heads and their bank balances were better than one. This worked well for some businesses: Ben and Jerry's, for one, and all those corner delis that seem to be called Three Guys Named Joe. But now the idea has lost its luster. If you've gone through the whole process of this book with someone else at your side, like we did, then perhaps a partnership would work; otherwise, don't risk it.

Why be wary of partners? Because the key to success in the 21st Century will be flexibility. Everything we talked about in Chapter Three will be seriously compromised if you find yourself checking with another person before making a decision. Everything we talked about in Chapter Three will be thrown away if you find yourself having to look after another person, should he turn out to be unstable for one reason or another. It's your idea, and you're bound to have certain, almost inexpressible, ideas about how you want the business to run. Your new partner will have a similar set of ideas, equally indefinable. In the undefined difference between the two will lie the seeds of your business's ruin. Sure, the extra investment would be wonderful, but we think it's just not worth the risk.

If you have no other choice, make sure that your combined abilities add up to more than the sum of their parts. Make sure one plus one equals three. And if you have a silent partner, make sure he or she stays silent, even when things aren't going well.

BANKS

As we hinted above, it's generally not the fault of the loan officer that he or she can't give you a loan to start your business. Banks have strict criteria that their employees need to meet when assigning loans. Banks generally like to see that you've been in business a year or two before giving you any money. They like to see that you have sufficient revenue to pay off the loan according to the terms they set. They also like to have some form of guarantee—your father-in-law's signature, for example.

Go and talk to your bank early on, anyway. Talk with the loan officer and see whether you can borrow just a small amount of money from them: even five hundred dollars would be good. Then you can pay it back and show them that you're a good credit risk. Don't alienate people if they reject you; you might need them later.

VENTURE CAPITALISTS

Somehow, somewhere, venture capitalists got a reputation for being daring, innovative white knights who rescue entrepreneurs in distress. Statistics show, however, that venture capitalists invest in less than three percent of all the new businesses that open every year. Like banks, they prefer to deal with more mature businesses. An investment from a venture capitalist is a mixed blessing in any case. While the extra money can help you expand the company, your actual percentage share of the business will probably drop into the single digits. Your influence on how the business is run will similarly diminish.

21ST CENTURY FINANCING

All of the following sources existed before the recession, but postrecession, we need to look at them in a new light. All of them have been, in one way or another, reinvigorated by the shake-up that the economic downturn gave them.

HOME EQUITY LOANS

We'll spend a great deal of time on home equity loans because, in our desire to be as pragmatic as possible, we're all but convinced that the vast majority of you who have actually come this far in the book will find them the best, perhaps even the only, option.

Home equity loans are going to be the most popular way for the 21st Century entrepreneur to raise start-up capital, simply because for most people their homes are the largest untapped resource available. Just as the Department of War was renamed the Department of Defense in order to polish its image, so second mortgages have been restyled as ''home equity loans.'' Nevertheless, since you're risking your major investment, your home, the home equity loan remains something to be entered into only after serious thought. However, you're not risking your home for something frivolous like a new stereo system or new carpet; you're starting a well-planned business, and you're going to budget paying the loan back in your financial plans. Just like the mortgage you already pay, a second mortgage is made up of two parts: a promise to pay back the money you borrow in certain amounts every month, and an agreement to give your property to the lender if you can't make the payments. You look for a home equity loan the same way you looked for your first mortgage.

Before you do anything, make sure your credit rating is accurate. You do this by calling the three major credit bureaus in

America and asking them where you should write to get a copy of your report. Here are their telephone numbers: TRW Credit Data, (214) 235-1200; Equifax/CBI, (404) 885-8000; and Trans-Union, (215) 569-4582. When you have a copy, make sure it's accurate. If you don't understand something, ask the agencies what it means. Ask your accountant whether any innocuous-sounding phrases are actually code words for something bad. We had an American Express card for a while but canceled it because we never used it. The way the cancellation was phrased on our report made it sound as though American Express had dropped us because we weren't paying our bills. If you do find an unexplainable error, ask the bureau about it. If they can't verify it, they must take it off your report. And check carefully—it's estimated that up to a quarter of the population has some mistake on their credit reports.

If your report is negative for a good reason (you once went bankrupt, for example), then you should explain how things have changed. Everyone is allowed to write a one-hundred-word note and have it attached to the report. Tell the truth; present yourself as a responsible citizen trying to correct past mistakes. If you were ill, or there was a death in your family, tell the credit bureau so. Conclude by saying how trustworthy you intend to be in the future.

Once your credit report is in good shape, then you can start to look for someone to lend you money. The advertisements in the real estate section of your Sunday paper are a good place to start. Then go to the yellow pages and look up "mortgages." You'll want to try credit unions, savings and loans, commercial banks, established finance companies, and mutual savings banks: any organization that does mortgages. Explain that you want to talk to a loan officer about a fixed-rate or adjustable-rate home equity loan.

The fastest way to decide whether the rates are good is to compare each lender's APR (annual percentage rate). This figure simplifies all the convoluted information and the confusing numbers that banks publicize. (It's usually the tiny number hidden at the bottom of the advertisement below all the good news!) Find out about fees: Sometimes these can swallow a lot of your loan.

It can make sense to take a slightly worse rate if you can avoid these up-front fees.

Watch out for "points." These are interest payments that you pay up front. One point means one percent of the principal at the time of the closing. They don't affect the amount of money that you pay overall, but you obviously want to pay as little as possible while you're struggling for money at the start of your business.

Check how much the rate will change—many variable-rate loans have limits (or "caps") on how much the rate can increase in one year, and during the length of the loan. Look at the fees and see how they'll add up over the years.

Talk to your accountant about whether you should get the type of loan in which you pay off some of the principal every month along with the interest (an amortizing loan), or one in which you just pay the interest and are faced with paying the principal at the end of the loan (a nonamortizing loan). If you can't pay that giant "balloon" payment, you either need to refinance (at more expense) or default on your loan, which means the bank takes your home.

If you've made some initial inquiries about the rates at a particular lending institution, and things look promising, gather the information on the following worksheet. By doing that, you'll keep a careful record of what the loan officer told you. The list looks like a lot of information to collect, but all of it is readily available to any loan officer, and you're only going to fill out the form for the lenders with the most promising rates. The bank may give you a number of options. Call them plan A, B, C, and so on.

Mortgage Company

_____

Name of loan officer

_____

Address

_____

Telephone number

_____

	Plan A	Plan B	Plan C
Fixed-Rate Loans			
Interest rate	_____	_____	_____
Points	_____	_____	_____
Origination fee	_____	_____	_____
Loan term	_____	_____	_____
Loan-to-value ratio	_____	_____	_____
Annual percentage rate	_____	_____	_____
Adjustable-Rate Loans			
Interest rate	_____	_____	_____
Adjustment period	_____	_____	_____
Index	_____	_____	_____
Adjustment period cap	_____	_____	_____
Lifetime cap	_____	_____	_____
Convertible	_____	_____	_____
If yes, when?	_____	_____	_____
Cost to convert	_____	_____	_____
Loan term	_____	_____	_____
Points	_____	_____	_____
Origination fee	_____	_____	_____
Loan-to-value (LTV)	_____	_____	_____
Annual percentage rate	_____	_____	_____

	Plan A	Plan B	Plan C
All Loans			
Nonincome verification	_____	_____	_____
Nonstandard LTV	_____	_____	_____
Debt-to-income ratio	_____	_____	_____
Application fee	_____	_____	_____
Appraisal fee	_____	_____	_____
Credit check fee	_____	_____	_____
Credit bureau used	_____	_____	_____
Bank attorney fee	_____	_____	_____
Prepayment penalty	_____	_____	_____
If yes, when?	_____	_____	_____
Cost to prepay	_____	_____	_____
Processing time	_____	_____	_____
Length of commitment	_____	_____	_____
Commitment renewable	_____	_____	_____
If yes, same rate?	_____	_____	_____
New rate	_____	_____	_____
Procedure	_____	_____	_____
Rate lock-in?	_____	_____	_____
If yes,			
at application	_____	_____	_____
at closing			
cost?	_____	_____	_____
Special programs	_____	_____	_____
Preferred customer benefits	_____	_____	_____

Documentation Required with Application

	Plan A	Plan B	Plan C
Fees	_____	_____	_____
Pay stub	_____	_____	_____
Tax returns	_____	_____	_____
Profit-and-loss statement	_____	_____	_____

	Plan A	Plan B	Plan C
Co-ops and condos:			
Contract of sale	_____	_____	_____
Offering plan	_____	_____	_____
Proprietary lease and bylaws	_____	_____	_____

For co-ops and two-family dwellings:			
Building financials	_____	_____	_____
Other	_____	_____	_____

Once you've chosen your second mortgage, fill out an application. These applications are fairly complex, because the institutions are trying to find out whether or not you're a good risk. Make yourself look as good as possible without lying.

You'll find there often isn't enough space on the form to put all the information you want. Surprisingly, this is deliberate on the part of the banks. They want short answers that can be coded by clerks and turned into numbers or "scored." At the end of the application, your score will be added up and you will or won't be awarded the loan.

The key to bypassing this scoring system is to give more information than one clerk has time or responsibility for. You shouldn't do this with unnecessary padding, but by providing full typewritten answers on a separate piece of paper. When faced with this, most clerks must pass the application on to a supervisor, who can use more discretion. And, you can use the extra space to explain anything that might appear odd to someone unfamiliar with your life. For example, your jobs may have forced you to move around a lot during the last few years. Or changing jobs frequently may be the norm in your field of work.

You've put a lot of effort into making this second mortgage application look good. Make the most of it now and make an appointment with the loan officer you've been talking to. Even if you're told to drop it in the mail, put on your interview clothes and go down to the bank. Ask for any loan officer and, in a matter-of-fact manner, explain that yours is a special application. Show the attached sheets and explain how you've cleaned up your credit (if you had to). Ask the officer to please guide the application through the procedure. The point of all this is that you'll have become a person to the bank, and as we all know, it's harder to reject a person than a piece of paper.

Of course, the bank may still reject you. In that case you're entitled by law to know why. Ask your new friend at the bank whether your application would be accepted if you cleared up that problem. Clear up the problem and appeal the decision. If you can see it's not working, go back to your worksheets and find another bank. Someone out there wants your money!

When you do find a bank, go over the contract with your lawyer before you sign anything. Sort out all the details. Ask any questions you have. You may not like to show your ignorance in front of others, but you'll feel much more stupid if it turns out that you've signed something rashly.

Let's look at some alternative forms of financing. The possible sources of financing are limited only by your imagination.

GOLDEN HANDSHAKES, PARACHUTES, AND KISS-OFFS

Previous employers are going to be popular sources of financing for those who become 21st Century entrepreneurs after losing a corporate job. We've already mentioned how one of the principals of The Advertising Partnership financed his share of the business with the money from his former Madison Avenue agency employer. Others have had similar positive experiences. Illustrator Anna Walker, for one. She worked full-time for a company for a year before it decided to move to the West Coast. Rather than try and relocate the staff, it just fired everyone. "It was actually a good thing," she says. "The severance money tided me over for a few months until I could show people my work and get enough jobs on my own."

If you leave on a positive note, you might even find you're able to sell your services right back to the company you just left: Presumably you aren't completely dispensable. You may even be able to negotiate some kind of free-lance contract as part of your severance deal. Choose to take the promise of work instead of money, because work is open-ended; a onetime cash settlement ends when the money's spent.

Just on a philosophical note, we think there's something poetic, even inspirational, about using a severance package to start your own business. What could be a more damaging blow to your confidence than being laid off? And yet what could be a more positive statement of self-confidence than starting your own business? We can think of nothing that more typifies the entrepreneurial spirit than taking your final paycheck and confidently investing it in your own future.

YOUR SUPPLIERS AND CUSTOMERS

Don't hesitate to ask your major clients and suppliers for help. If you know suppliers well enough and they are convinced your business has a fighting chance of succeeding, then they may be willing to give you some supplies and wait a month till you've sold them before charging you. And if your clients have enough faith in your abilities, they may be willing to pay you an advance on work you've yet to perform. For our newsletter, for example, we convinced our printer to wait a month before charging us for the paper; the post office obviously wasn't so obliging. Some service businesses are ideally suited to this kind of arrangement: It would not be at all unreasonable for a service business like a garden landscape firm to ask to be paid in installments as the work progressed. The customer might even appreciate being able to spread out the bill.

YOUR FAMILY AND FRIENDS

In small groups, take your family and friends quickly through the process you went through to arrive at your choice of business. (Go over it individually with those people who have the most money.) Ask them for whatever financial help they can provide you with. You may not need to sell yourself to them—they already have confidence in you, we hope—but you do need to show them what you're doing and why. Explain that you'll work out whatever terms they want. Offer to pay them back (with or without interest) steadily, a little bit every month. (Don't forget to write this into your business checklist as part of your working capital's fixed costs.) Or offer to give them a percentage of the profits, which is more exciting, potentially more rewarding, and definitely more risky (for them). Remind them that everyone thought that Alec Guinness was crazy when he agreed to be paid a percentage of the profits of an oddball sci-fi movie called *Star Wars*. This is the kind of loan that you want them to give you. But be careful not to give away eleven promises of ten percent. Always give family members a formal letter explaining how you'll pay them back. Some people suggest going to grandparents and being frank with them, saying, "Listen, you've told us that you're going to leave us such and such in your will. Why not give it to us now when we really need it?" Clearly this approach wouldn't work with all grandparents—certainly not ours—but try it if you think it might work.

YOUR OWN MONEY

You'd be amazed at how much money you can save if you put your mind to it. Look back at our suggestions in Chapter Nine. Stop eating out. Cut down on your drinking. Don't buy any new clothes or compact disks. Disconnect your TV from cable TV. We went on a similar regime when saving to buy our apartment and managed to pile up four thousand dollars in about five months. Of course, we had to have a party once we'd moved in order to reintroduce ourselves to our friends, but we achieved our goals.

THE U.S. SMALL BUSINESS ADMINISTRATION

If you've been rejected by at least three other financial institutions, then you're allowed to go to the SBA and apply for a loan. There are several loan programs that your local office of the SBA can describe in detail. Some loans are geared to businesses requiring funding over one million dollars; others are for more modest needs. Various groups are also helped by the SBA. There are loans for minority-owned companies, energy loans, and handicapped assistance loans. Back before the recession, the SBA was seen as a last-ditch resource. Now people are feeling a little more comfortable about receiving government funding. And it is, after all, a loan, not welfare. There's a long waiting list and a whole bunch of paperwork to wade through before you can get a loan, but they are available. This might be something to work on right from the beginning, and if it comes through, see it as a windfall.

Another government initiative is "The Small Business Innovation Research Program (SBIR)," which directs the funds of national agencies like the Departments of Energy, Education, and Health to small business. Don't forget the business incubators we talked about in Chapter Eight.

INSURANCE POLICIES AND SUPPLEMENTAL RETIREMENT ANNUITIES

If you have an SRA, you can borrow against it at a very favorable rate. The gamble is, of course, that you might end up poverty-stricken at age sixty-five with no retirement fund. Similarly, with insurance policies, you have another source of financing, if you have enough in there to make it worth borrowing against. Just be aware of the risk you're taking, and talk to your accountant before you do anything rash.

FOUNDATIONS

The Horatio Alger myth of "making it in America" being as strong as it is, it's no wonder that there are foundations willing to award grants to people who want to start businesses. This isn't for everyone, of course—the criteria are very strict, and you need to be able to write a mind-blowingly good proposal in order to be considered. Check your local library for books about this and a directory of foundations.

ANGELS

Angels can be individuals or groups. They decide they want to help out local businesses and perhaps make some money on the side. It's a way of mixing philanthropy and gambling. Often you'll find angels are successful local business people who want to do something with their money and also pass on some of their knowledge. They won't be prepared, or able, to invest the millions that venture capitalists offer, but you don't want that much, and you'll find they'll often be more sympathetic because they've come from where you are. There are an estimated 250,000 angels out there, busy investing away in small companies. One estimate puts the total amount of money put up by angels at about five times that invested by venture capital companies. You just need to make sure you get along with them and that your angels remain fairly quiet. They'll want to give you advice, and you'll need to take some of it. Who knows? It may even turn out to be good.

Ask all your professionals whether they know of any such angels. Hang around at trade fairs again, schmooze, try people out, and whatever you do, don't be embarrassed: People love to be asked for help.

By using any one or a combination of these methods, you should be able to get on your feet. Raise the cash one thousand dollars at a time. Sell yourself well. Tell everyone how interested everyone else is. Do all you can to generate a little excitement. You know you're going to be big, so let other people in on the ground floor. Don't push or cajole, just lead them on a little at a time.

This is a difficult part of the process. You clearly want to be a self-reliant person—after all, that's one reason you want to be an entrepreneur. If you're like most entrepreneurs, you'd be more comfortable plunging right into your business rather than spending time trying to raise money. Bite the bullet and, if need be, your tongue. Be polite and civil to your potential backers for a few more weeks and soon you'll be off, running your own company. Meanwhile, consider how you're going to generate excitement and attract clients once the business actually exists. How are you going to market this service of yours? The next chapter explores some ways.

For more information on the topics covered in Chapter Eleven, take a look at the following books:

- *Directory of Money Sources for Small Business* (Gordon, 1992)
- *Free Money: For Small Businesses & Entrepreneurs,* by Laurie Blum (Wiley, 1989)
- *Raising Seed Money for Your Own Business,* by Brian Smith (Viking, 1984)
- *Start-Up Money: Raise What You Need for Your Small Business,* by Jennifer Lindsey (Wiley, 1989)

12

BUILD YOURSELF
AN EMPIRE

How Do You Get Your Clients' Attention?

Without giving ourselves too many delusions of grandeur, we've found attracting customers' attention—marketing—is best thought of as building an empire. You want to have control over as many people as possible, and you want them to give you money on a regular basis.

Some empires are more successful than others in maintaining their power, and in future chapters we will look at what you can learn from both the successes and failures. But first let's examine the best ways of putting together the empire, or conquering the market you're interested in. We'll look at all the work you've done so far and then explain the techniques you'll use in your assault on the general public.

It's important to begin with an understanding that marketing isn't only about advertising; there's a lot of research that has to be done before you call the newspapers. Fortunately, you did much of this research while following the suggestions in chapters Five, Six, and Seven. Let's review for a minute.

You've done market research by surveying late-twentieth-century America looking for markets that seemed likely to grow in the new century. Instead of trying to bend your business to current trends the way a large corporation like General Motors does, you've found a field that's taking off economically, and you're ready to go with it. Even better, you've found a field that interests you, so you know you'll remain excited and enthusiastic.

You found a niche back in Chapter Five by examining your

field carefully and doing some more detailed market research into what people would want from your service. You looked at magazines, you visited libraries, went to the SBA, and finally came up with a specific idea for your business, either by adapting someone else's idea or by coming up with one of your own. You found a segment of the market that's not being satisfied and you positioned yourself to fill it.

You've identified your customers by deciding whether to sell to businesses or to individuals. You know where they are, and from all your previous research, you know what kind of buying habits they have. In Chapter Six you went over all your notes and arguments to make sure you weren't making any hasty decisions. You even did some market research about your potential rivals so you could position yourself differently from them. And in Chapter Ten you worked out what the price of your service should be, having taken into account your financial needs.

Now you need to do the parts of marketing that will actually get the service sold. This is called the market mix. It's made up of four areas: promotion, distribution, advertising, and publicity. Promotion is those things you use to make a special impression, whatever the media involved. Distribution is how you deliver your product or service to a client or customer. Advertising consists of whatever you do on a regular basis to let people know about your service. Publicity is information about you coming from someone other than yourself, thus making it seem unbiased. These four areas have been marketing's four major weapons for the last fifty years. Even though newer ideas are superseding them (ideas that we'll explore in the next chapter), it's worth looking at the best of the old ideas before moving on. We'll concentrate on how the major media and techniques can grab people's attention and help you to build your empire. We will leave out distribution since, for most service businesses, that really isn't part of marketing, and we will also leave direct mail for the next chapter.

ADVERTISING AND PROMOTION

Advertising and promotion are so closely allied that it makes sense to discuss them together. Promotion can be thought of as one-shot advertising.

PRINT ADVERTISING

Print advertising is important in that it's equally good at both regular advertising and special promotions. In Chapter Six you researched which newspapers your competitors use to advertise. Don't just stop there; think about what other magazines, journals, and newspapers your clients might read. If you think you might get a lot of churchgoers as customers, advertise in the monthly parish newspaper. We'll get into the advantages and disadvantages of various types of publications in a few paragraphs, but we wanted to first offer some general advice about print advertising.

Speak with advertising representatives from a variety of publications. They can explain their publications' unique reader demographics, try to show how that matches your clients' demographic profile, and tell you about costs. Feel free to try to make a deal; you've nothing to lose. Most publications, though they are loath to admit it, have more than one rate scale. Make sure you sign a contract, and ask whether there are any bulk-buying discounts, or discounts for advertising on standby—if a space opens up, your ad is used to fill it.

See if you can design your own ads; it'll save you money. But be honest with yourself—if the result looks lousy, pay someone else to do it. Many publications will prepare an ad for you for a nominal fee. Always be conscious of the kind of image you want to project. We will talk more about this in the next chapter, but you want to try to escape from the kind of bludgeoning that has been the norm over the last half century. So don't write "Buy Now!!!! Only $9.99!!!" You want to project calm assurance, not desperation.

Think about where in the publication you want the ads to run, and how often. Running them regularly is a good idea, preferably in the same location, unless you're tying the advertisement in to a special promotion and you think it would be better to put it in a specific section. Check whether there will be any special advertising supplements that focus on particular markets, like weddings, vacations, or decorating. Since each type of magazine or newspaper advertisement has its advantages and disadvantages, you'll need to work out what combination best suits your business.

Now let's take a look at the various types of publications out there clamoring for your limited advertising dollars.

DAILY AND WEEKLY NEWSPAPERS

By placing an ad in a daily newspaper, you're meeting fresh people every day, but people usually only read the paper once. You probably can't afford to catch a consumer's eye with a large, full-page ad, so you need to advertise regularly, in the same place. Your potential clients need to know where to look for you. In addition to the more traditional classified ads, some papers group similar businesses in directories that are printed among the feature articles. Because these are more likely to be seen by the casual reader than are the classified ads, they're worth the extra money. Don't clutter up your ad with too much information or small type: It won't reproduce well in newsprint.

Many towns and cities have weekly newspapers aimed at a particular group. These papers are kept around longer and are often read more thoroughly than a daily paper, simply because they address the particular interests of the reader. Once again, a regularly placed ad is the best way to get attention. If people need your service, they'll remember that they saw your ad last week and dig the paper out of the recycling bin, or look for your ad the next week. Position your ads toward groups that are buying these special-interest papers. But don't go overboard: Unless you know the habits and humor of the culture well, don't try to be amusing; you may be seen as an outsider trying to muscle your way in. Your clients are sharp enough to know when you're striking a false note.

Don't overlook the free newspapers that are left in the front of supermarkets and coffee shops. They're read more widely and thoroughly than you might expect, and their rates compare favorably with more established daily or weekly newspapers.

CONSUMER MAGAZINES

There are three kinds of consumer magazines: general interest, special interest, and regional. All are aimed at individuals as opposed to businesses.

General-interest magazines try to appeal to as many people as possible. *Time* is a classic example of a magazine that is read by all sorts of people in all sorts of places. You wouldn't be surprised to see it both in a dentist's waiting room and on your grandmother's coffee table. Some general-interest magazines try to make their readership a little more focused. *Vanity Fair* and *The Star* cover the same topics, for example—gossip, fashion, and the lives of the rich and famous—but are designed to appeal to very different readers. Of course, having such a wide readership allows these magazines to charge a lot for their premium advertising space. However, the classified ads are often reasonably priced and worth spending your money on. Ask the magazine representatives who their readers are and see whether those demographics match your needs. But think carefully about who your customers are going to be, and whether yours is the sort of service that people are going to look for in the classified ads.

Special-interest magazines cater, obviously, to enthusiasts. A quick glance at the racks of any newsstand will show you the diversity of America's hobbies. It's almost a certainty that there's at least one magazine about your business or some part of it. (If not, consider starting one, just as we did with our iguana newsletter!) Most of the special-interest magazines don't have as high a circulation as the general-interest magazines, but if the subject matches the service you're selling, then you've found an ideal place to advertise. Also consider advertising in magazines whose readers have interests indirectly related to your service. For example, if your service is organizing backpacking vacations, then consider advertising in magazines that cater to related sports, like mountain biking or skiing. There are bound to be people who ski and hike. You can go even further: *Premiere,* for instance, styles itself as a magazine for movie enthusiasts, but it carries ads for expensive cars, liquor, diamond rings, and music, as well as those you'd expect for movies and videos. The advertisers know that *Premiere* has a sophisticated readership, with money to spend on luxuries.

Regional magazines are sort of a cross between the other two types. Their content often mirrors general-interest magazines in their range, but the information is specialized in that every story has a local angle. Their circulation, while generally lower than the general-interest publications, depends to a large extent on the population of the region they are covering. *Arizona Highways,* for instance, has a smaller circulation than *New York,* simply because there are fewer people in the whole state of Arizona than there are in the New York City metropolitan area. If your service is aimed at people living in your town, then you'd be wasting your time spending money on an ad in *Newsweek.* Of course, if you live in a large city, then the magazine's readership may well be in the hundreds of thousands anyway.

Most areas, even very small cities, have a weekly-listings magazine that covers everything going on in town. This is often a good place to advertise because people refer back to it again and again during the week. If you advertise regularly in the same place in the weekly-listings magazine, people will know where to look up your phone number. You'll have, in effect, created a miniature billboard.

TRADE MAGAZINES

These are aimed at businesses rather than consumers. This is well illustrated by comparing *Premiere* with *Variety.* The former is designed for people who go to movies, while the latter is designed for people who make movies. Trade magazines have a relatively small circulation compared to the consumer magazines, even though a subscription is often free to those in the business being addressed. That's because they're generally very tightly targeted. And even though the trades make their money on advertising rather than subscriptions, rates tend to be affordable.

Trade magazines are often very specific. For example, while there are some trade magazines for restaurant owners in general, there are even more for each specific type of restaurant, ranging from bistro to pizza parlor. There are literally thousands of these magazines, some devoted to subjects outsiders find obscure but insiders find essential. And most important from your point of view, there is never just one magazine for an industry. (Remember the copycat principle.) For instance, people who work with coin-operated machines have three magazines to go to for up-to-the-

minute information: *American Coin-op, Play Meter Magazine,*
and *Vending Times.* In the very specialized publications, due to
the cutthroat competition for a small group of potential advertisers, rates are often very negotiable, and advertiser service is
stressed. Trade publications are famous, or infamous, for being
very agreeable to running favorable news stories about their advertisers. At the very least they'll happily publicize whatever
you'd like in exchange for some advertising. Clearly these magazines are invaluable places to advertise for those who are selling
to businesses.

Newsletters

If you're looking for a really well-defined consumer audience,
you should consider advertising in newsletters. They're sort of
the consumer equivalent of trade magazines. When you run a spot
in a newsletter, you'll know precisely who's reading your ad. The
economics of newsletters, though, is the reverse of trade publications: They rely on subscriptions for their money. Some newsletters regularly carry ads; others may not even have thought about
it. Call the editors of all the promising newsletters and ask whether
they accept advertising. Some newsletters won't want to run ads
for fear of people thinking their editorial independence might be
influenced. Most, however, will be eager for any extra source of
income. You've seen the tight budget that *RIFP* is on. Even though
we aren't planning to solicit advertising until we get more of a
sense of our audience, we'd be overjoyed to have someone call
us up and offer to advertise with us. Make sure to ask to see a copy
of the newsletter before you commit, and sign a contract—some
newsletters may be so amateurish, they'd do more harm than good
for your image.

Telephone Directories

Telephone directories are crucial places for a small service
business to advertise. They are the first place many people turn
to find some service providers. And those who are looking at your
ad are doing so for a reason. In effect, your audience here is
already sold on the service itself; they just haven't decided who

to hire. Your goal in your ad, therefore, is to give them reasons for calling or stopping by. Pay for a box ad rather than an enlarged alphabetical listing. You don't need graphics—text should suffice. If clients come to you, make sure your location is clear. (Describe a cross street, landmark, or big store that you're near, as well as giving your address.) If you visit the customer, say so explicitly. A black background with your business's name "cut out" is the most eye-catching combination, much better than paying for a different color or putting a fussy border around the ad. If you have the space and money, stating the obvious won't do you any harm. Saying something like "Polite, efficient service every time" or "Call for a free estimate" will give you an edge over your neighbor on the page.

The major problem with telephone directories is that people often don't know how to look up the business they want. Finding a plumber is simple—you look up "plumbing." But things often get complicated: Even to rent a car, you need to make a leap to "auto rental." If you want to buy lawn furniture, you won't find it under "lawn," you need to look up "garden and lawn furnishings," "furniture manufacturers," and "furniture outdoors." We had an antique clock we wanted to have appraised. It took most of a morning, looking up numbers in the directory under "clock service and repair," "clock dealers," "insurance," "appraisers," "antiques dealers," "art galleries dealers and consultants," and "auctioneers," before we found someone who could do it. The solution is to place an ad in every category in which someone might look for you. And make the services you offer clear in the ad itself: Don't assume clients will call for elaboration.

FLIERS AND POSTERS

Fliers and posters are the cheapest ways to promote your service, and often, the more you order, the cheaper it gets. Generally they are more effective for promotions rather than regular advertising since they aren't substantial enough to make more than a momentary impact. Produce the poster or flier on a computer with a simple clean design and a frame around the edge. Make sure your telephone number or address is clearly displayed. Put rip-off numbers on the bottom if that would help. Think carefully about where you put the posters. Community bulletin boards at supermarkets, churches, and temples are always good places, but be a little imaginative in terms of both place and time. How about the corner where all the mothers wait for the children to come out of school? How about by the stairs at the train station? People are always going in and out of hair salons and dry cleaners, so if the owners will let you, these are good places to put laminated, slightly more permanent posters. Go back regularly and check that the posters are still up.

The disadvantages of fliers and posters are that they can become tattered very quickly, and they may not project the kind of image that you want. So if you do choose to use them, when you walk around the neighborhood, make sure you rip down any scruffy posters (we mean your own).

You will probably need to pay someone to stand and hand fliers to people, unless you can twist your son's or daughter's arm. Make a (light) sandwich board with your name and number on the front and back for the distributor to wear. Promise your kid a bonus if you see him or her smiling whenever you come by.

BROADCAST ADVERTISING

By *broadcast advertising* we mean advertising that is transmitted electronically. It's more fleeting than print advertising, but if used well, it can have a great impact on potential clients. For most small businesses, broadcast has often been more associated with promotion than regular advertising due to its high cost. But as newspaper and magazine readership in general drops, it's become more and more common to turn to the broadcast media for regular advertising. This has evolved into sponsorship of a particular show or event, such as the 10:30 A.M. stock market report on the radio, or the 11:25 weather report on the local cable news program. Actually, television used to be out of the question for all but the most affluent businesses. But today, with the proliferation of cable channels, rates are starting to drop.

RADIO ADVERTISING

Radio is a peculiar business. Unlike a newspaper ad, a radio spot is there and then it's gone: The customer can't refer back to it for information. As a result, announcing telephone numbers and addresses isn't a great idea, unless you've paid extra for some kind of 1-800-I*G*U*A*N*A*S number. The best thing you can do in a radio ad is to try to be humorous, and repeat your business's name frequently. If you do give your address, describe where you are, as you did in the telephone directory, rather than just giving the street address. Work with the ad representatives at the radio station to find someone who can write your script with you. And pay someone with a "radio" voice to read it, unless you're deliberately trying for a hokey, Frank Perdue effect. People tend to listen to the radio at the same time every day, so if you can identify when your customers might be listening, then only pay for air time then. For example, if you run a travel agency, you should advertise during the station's travel show.

There are also many specialized radio stations catering to particular ethnic or age groups. It might make sense to advertise on one of these. But whatever you do, don't waste your money on the cheap 3:00 A.M. time slot: It's cheap because absolutely no one's listening.

It's better to advertise every day for two weeks rather than once a week for fourteen weeks. That way you make yourself heard above the "noise" of all the other ads. Plus, radio is probably still best used for short-term promotions, when you want to give some special offer or sale an extra boost. Then you can tell people to look for the ad in the paper for more details.

TELEVISION ADVERTISING

Our opinion is that, for the moment, small businesses should stay away from TV advertising. This goes for local and cable television as well as the already too expensive networks. Soon cable television technology will be sophisticated enough to allow advertisers to send their commercials exclusively to potential customers. If this results in lower costs, then it may become worth your while to use cable. Currently it's just not worth it: You'll pay a lot of money for indifferent results.

If you do decide to use television, don't think you can lower costs by cutting corners in production. Trying to save money by skimping on any part of the process is a surefire recipe for disaster. For some reason, low-budget commercials are inevitably underlit and marred by poor sound. They just give everyone the impression your business is a second-class affair, and that's the last thing you want. Another problem is one of context: If you choose to advertise late at night, your commercial will be sandwiched between a pitch for the Garden Weasel and do-it-yourself swimming pools. If you choose to advertise in prime time, you'll only be able to afford one thirty-second spot, and even then you'll be sandwiched between million-dollar productions or, worse, tacked onto the end of a series of commercials, by which time the last thing the viewer will want to see is yet another ad, especially a poor-quality one. If you can afford a sophisticated commercial that will be shown when people are actually going to be watching, then go ahead—find a professional production company and do it. Otherwise forget about advertising on television.

PUBLICITY

Publicity is an unbiased or indirect endorsement of your business. The best form is word of mouth. Some pundits are even suggesting that the only point of using advertising in the 21st Century will be to generate good word-of-mouth publicity. People don't trust advertising as much as they once did, these pundits say, so they look to their friends and colleagues to advise them. There's a great deal of truth to this notion. The next time you're at a party, ask if anyone knows the name of a good dentist, and we guarantee you'll be deluged with people recommending their own dentists and warning you off others.

Word of mouth can be generated, if you make a conscious effort at it. Whenever you finish with clients, ask them if they're satisfied. If they are, ask them to recommend you to their friends, colleagues, and co-workers. When you get new customers or clients, ask them how they heard of you. It's not a rude question, unless you make it sound as though they're not the kind of customers you're looking for. If the new client was recommended through word of mouth, you have someone in common to talk about (but don't get drawn into gossip). Next time you see the recommender, thank him or her for the good word of mouth—it will make it seem as though your relationship goes beyond money (more on this in the next chapter) and will encourage additional recommendations. Establish a mailing list of all your clients, and regularly send them information about sales and special offers for "special clients."

Graphic designer Gregg Trueman has found another great way to get good word-of-mouth publicity. "By teaching new techniques, I find clients and other people through the classes. It doesn't pay much, but I get my name in the catalog, and that spreads it around." A variation on Trueman's technique is to become a sponsor of noncommercial events or activities. For instance, sponsorship of a Little League team guarantees a certain amount of public goodwill and, since the name of your business is printed on the uniforms, you'll be visible to every parent who comes to the games. The same is true for sponsoring charitable events. You could also teach a class at the local adult ed center or community college, or volunteer to speak in front of local clubs.

Another excellent form of publicity is getting a mention in the media. Elysa Lazar, publisher of *Sales and Bargains Reports,* says that for a 21st Century entrepreneur, this is the only way to go, and that "getting mentioned in *The New York Times* was worth any amount of paid advertising." That's because a media mention is seen as an unbiased endorsement of you as an expert. Even if you're just mentioned briefly in a round-up of similar services, it still appears to be an endorsement by the paper. It's up to you to try and make the mention more than just a mention: You must stand out from the competition. (We'll talk more about this in the next chapter.) You can solicit such media coverage. Get into the habit of sending out well-written, confident press releases to all the relevant media. Emphasize any genuinely new or different services you offer. Talk about what makes your company unique.

Remember, editors and journalists want to believe they're reporting a real story, not just doing your public relations.

Corky Pollan, editor of the "Best Bets" shopping column in *New York Magazine,* receives hundreds of press releases every week, of which only two or three are of interest to her. She told us that it's very important that a release be concise; less than a page, in fact. All the information should be there, mostly in the first or second paragraphs—no one should need to call to find out how much the service costs or when you're open. If it's appropriate, send a picture as well. Pollan finds that people sometimes misspell names—even hers—in their press releases. (She has received mail addressed to Mr. Korky Pollen, Cirky Polan, and Korky Pollit.) The moral is, proofread your release carefully. At the top of the page, put the name and number of someone the editor or writer can contact, just in case more information is needed.

Do offer to show the writer or editor around your office if he wants to visit. Make time to talk to him, even if you don't have the time. Find out when he needs the information and schedule a time to talk, even if you end up calling him one evening. If you do advertise in the publication, don't mention it to the editor or reporter. That will be seen as a not-so-subtle blackmail attempt. Rest assured that, if it's possible, the ad rep at the paper has already spoken to the reporter. When the piece has run, send a thank-you note; you'd be surprised at the number of businesses that clamor for attention before the plug, then complain afterwards. They usually don't get written about again. If you develop a good enough relationship with a journalist or editor, you might find yourself called on to give your opinion as an expert in your field, and that's hitting the publicity jackpot.

Most professionals and consultants are going to find that publicity is, in fact, the only advertising they can do. No one really trusts lawyers and doctors who advertise on television. In addition to making speeches, the publicity-minded professional should write articles for relevant trade magazines. Articles are easier to do than they look. Just find a subject that appeals to you, do some research, and write it. If you aren't confident about your writing ability, have someone else work on it with you. Magazines and newspapers are desperate for new ideas, and all of them have editors whose job it is to improve your lousy writing. If they like your article, they'll work on it until it's printable. If you find writing comes easily, you should consider writing a book. This won't make you much money, but it will make you an instant expert.

Yet another way to become an expert is to teach. As the 21st Century approaches, all community colleges and universities are looking for people who will add a touch of the real world to their curricula. They won't pay you a lot for sharing this information, and you don't want it to take up too much of your time, but teaching is an excellent way to make people recognize your name. Also, newspapers and television stations often look to the local colleges when they need an expert. It sounds more impressive to declare, "Alfredo Marx, lecturer in applied economics at Texas State, says ..." rather than "Alfredo Marx, consultant, says ...." The point being that teaching a subject makes you an instant authority.

PUTTING IT ALL TOGETHER

Let's go over some general guidelines for pulling all these disparate elements together into a 21st Century marketing program. First of all, it's a good idea to use more than one medium at a time. Try to have some constant advertising using whichever combination of the following makes the most sense: a telephone directory ad, a regular newspaper ad, fliers, and posters. If you have a great deal of money, you could add a regular radio sponsorship to the mix. Otherwise, use radio from time to time to promote special events. Tie in radio with other promotional ads, such as an enlarged and different newspaper ad, or a special blitz of fliers and posters. Similarly, use publicity for both regular and promotional marketing. Actively encourage and reward word of mouth. Combine special-event press releases with ongoing reminders of regular events to keep your name in front of the media. Whenever you're approached for a quote or information, go out of your way to be helpful and opinionated. That way you'll become a regular source. Look for noncommercial opportunities to put your face and name in the public eye. Finally, remember that marketing isn't an exact art, it's a hit-and-miss affair that needs constant attention and fine-tuning. So work at it steadily and try to perfect your skills.

RIFP MARKETS!

At *RIFP* we decided to put a small ad in four special-interest pet magazines and monitor which got the most response. When we knew which was the most productive magazine, we placed a slightly larger ad in it. We paid our nephew to hand out fliers outside the local pet stores, and we put up posters in every pet store in the city. We labeled some of our newsletters "complimentary copy" and left them in local pet stores. We asked the store owners to give one to each customer who buys an iguana. In exchange, we gave each of the stores a small ad in the newsletter. We rented booths at pet shows where we set ourselves up as experts and gave away more free copies of our newsletter. We took along our two peg iguanas, Iggy and Squiggy, put them on leashes, and took turns walking them around the hall. We even ran off a few hundred buttons with the phrase "Take a reptile home to meet the kids!" and handed them out for free. Finally, we sponsored a Little League team, the Brooklyn Iguanas.

⊰⊱ 13 ⊰⊱

HOLD ON TO YOUR EMPIRE

Keeping Your Customers Satisfied

Up until about five years ago, using the techniques we outlined in the last chapter might have been enough to let you stay in business. However, things have changed. There are new rules of warfare, and you'll need to know them in order to survive and flourish in the 21st Century. Ironically, the best way to understand what has happened is to examine past empires. As Santayana said, "Those who cannot remember the past are condemned to repeat it."

When it comes to marketing your service, you can choose to emphasize brute force or intellectual and emotional persuasion. You're going to need both force and persuasion, but we'll convince you that to be successful in the 21st Century, you'll need to rely mostly on persuasion. The last chapter taught you some of the useful brute-force techniques. This chapter will teach you how to convince people emotionally and intellectually that yours is the service to choose.

Force vs. Choice is an age-old battle, which has been played out again and again throughout history: Sparta versus Athens, the Mongol hordes versus the Romans, the Vikings versus the Anglo-Saxons, Britain versus Revolutionary America, Nazi Germany versus the Allies, and the Soviet Union versus Western Europe. If you look back on all these historic examples, you'll find that initially the aggressive, warmongering cultures seemed to do well against the more intellectual, democratic cultures, often seeming to eclipse them, but sooner or later the ideas of the more sophisticated, choice-based society rose again and influenced the invaders.

We don't study the Mongol contribution to world civilization at college. Nazi Germany and Stalin's Soviet Union are interesting to study, but not because of their positive contributions to humanity. They're studied because of the lessons we can learn from their failures.

If you want to be a long-lasting, successful empire builder, you should follow the lead of the Romans. You must make people believe they are better off being ruled by you. There's a great scene in Monty Python's *Life of Brian* in which the leader of the Judean People's Front asks what the imperialist Romans have ever done for them. "The aqueduct?" someone suggests. "The streets are safe," says someone else. "And don't forget wine," another yells. The list grows longer and longer, and their revolutionary zeal appears increasingly pointless. The Pythons were making a good point: The best way to keep people happy is to give them what they want. Brute force can win people over for short periods of time, but it's impossible to keep it up forever, as the British found out in 1776.

This all applies directly to marketing your business. We're coming to the end of a period of aggression and bullying when marketers and ad agencies thought the only way to win the allegiance of customers was by hounding them mercilessly. This era began in earnest with the spread of television in the forties. Before this, advertising was essentially local. There were syndicated radio shows, national magazines, and even some nationwide billboard campaigns, but in order to sell a product, you essentially went to an area and developed a local campaign. Suddenly, with the advent of television, companies could reach the entire nation at once, and taking full advantage of this, they descended upon the population of America like a plague. And it worked . . . for a while.

The logic behind the television sales pitch ran like this: If a company is big enough to advertise to the whole nation, then it must be making a profit. And if it's making a profit, then a lot of people must be buying its products. And if so many people are buying its products, then the products must be good. While all of this was true in some cases, the flaw in the logic was that a company with enough capital could just buy the advertising and con people into thinking the rest of the argument followed. With only a minute in which to advertise their products, the marketers had to convince people quickly. They used three basic lines: "Buy this and become the person in the commercial," "This is a bargain," and "This is new and better!" To try to compete, the print and radio ads began to use the same techniques. There was less explaining and convincing and more "Be like this!" The poor consumers had no choice but to listen to the advertisers. Consumers could believe or disbelieve, but when faced with a choice on Main Street, they tended to go for the name they recognized. This worked well for about fifty years.

Then something happened. At some point during the late seventies, when over 90 percent of the nation owned a television set, the aggressive success of the advertising world began to falter. All the different messages began to blend together, and consumers felt deafened by the noise. Then, to the horror of the advertisers, consumers began to ignore the noise. At first Madison Avenue responded with brighter colors, better graphics, and more sex. This worked for a while in the eighties, but the net effect was merely to generate more noise. Then the advertisers turned to self-referential commercials, in which they made fun of other commercials. The Energizer Bunny was the most popular example of this. The hidden message behind this kind of ad was "Hey, listen, we hate ads, too. Look, we're all laughing at stupid ads together; you can identify with us and our product. We're different because we aren't going to try and pull the wool over your eyes." Except, of course, they were trying to pull the wool over our eyes while positioning themselves as rebels. This worked for a while, but then it was imitated too many times and became swallowed up by the noise. Right now advertising agencies are confused and upset. They can't find a way to differentiate the products they are supposed to be selling. All the print liquor ads look the same. All the television car commercials look the same. If one company does come up with something new, it's immediately copied by other companies, which takes away the original's power.

And this is where the 21st Century entrepreneur comes in. You're taking up a principle that was too readily thrown aside in the middle of the century. People will be ready to welcome you back, although they'll be confused to begin with and will wonder whether you're sincere about your promises. But you're going to win them over by giving them real, quality service.

HOW TO WIN FRIENDS AND INFLUENCE PEOPLE

The consumer has rebelled against the bullies of the television era. The consumer won't be threatened anymore and won't be dazzled by newer and better visual pyrotechnics. Any business that doesn't grasp this fundamental change is going to go under fairly quickly. This is where you take the lead. You're going to go back to the forties, back to a time when the customer could buy something without the influence of television. You're going to build a relationship with your customer. We don't mean this as a metaphor, we mean it as a fact: Your business is going to be a friend to its customers. The old-style corner barber knew everyone who came into his shop, and if he didn't know you, he'd get to know you little by little. He wouldn't call you by your first name to start with, and he wouldn't be overly friendly, he'd let the relationship evolve naturally. If a regular customer didn't come into the shop for a long time, he'd call him up to make sure he wasn't sick. He'd always have a lollipop for a kid and he'd always ask how business was going. This is the kind of relationship you're going to build with your customers. Once you begin, you'll find it gets easier and easier. Once you have this relationship, then you'll be perceived as giving good value for money. When you give good value, and customers know it and talk about it, you'll be a success.

Here are four methods you'll use to build a relationship with your clients and customers.

BE PROACTIVE

Many businesses claim they respond to the needs of their customers, but what they really mean is, they give their customers a limited choice and say, "Which would you prefer?" You're going to react to the needs of your clients, but you're going to go one step further. You're going to react to their needs before they even know they have them. That's being proactive. It sounds impossible, but it can be done. You need to know your customers very well and you need to be completely involved with your customers and your business. This is one of the reasons we made sure you were enthusiastic about the field when you chose the business.

One of America's leading experts on this kind of marketing is Joel Tucciarone at a company called Zoetics. He calls this idea of forming a relationship with the customer *relational marketing*. "Relational marketing," he says, "is putting the customer at the center of your business and allowing the customer to be the change agent." The consumer won't ever need to say, "Could you do this for me?" You'll have already thought of it. How are you going to get to know your customers well enough to predict their needs? After all, you can't just say you want to be their friend.

Think back to when you were a child in school. If you wanted to make friends, you couldn't appear desperate. You couldn't just walk up to someone and say, "I want to be your friend, please, please, please." No, you had to do it another way. Teachers and child psychologists agree the best way to gain acceptance by the group is to "acquire mutual experiences"; that is, to do things together. You must wait for the right moment. Like a child, hang around on the edge of the group for a while without betraying any signs of desperation. Groups spend most of their time doing the same old things because there's comfort in familiarity. Most of the time, they don't want to try anything new—like your friendship, for instance. Eventually the right moment comes along. The key is to wait until something exciting occurs, a moment when the focus of the group suddenly goes from itself to something outside. Now, for children, this might be chasing a dog, hitting a tree with a stick, or playing a game of touch football. For adults this would be something that breaks the routine, like the Fourth of July weekend, the opening of a new cinema in town, the homecoming parade, or a visit by someone famous. When the focus moves away from the concerns of a group itself, that's your chance to join, almost unnoticed. For your business, this might mean being a sponsor of the fireworks display or offering to cater the homecoming picnic.

By doing this, you've joined the group in a nonthreatening way, you've become part of people's lives. Now, all of this also takes place on two levels. On the everyday level, you'll get to know your customers by talking to them, by being one of them. Ask them what they want, and don't just get what they specifically ask for, but go to the higher level and become proactive: Think about what else they might want. Let's say you run a gift-buying service. If someone wants you to pick up a gift for her grandmother, see if she wants you to get a card too. Even find out whether there's a place where Grandma can return the gift in her hometown if she doesn't like it.

This thinking ahead is what Gregg Trueman is doing at Neo-Graphics. In his business of graphic design, he's forced to think ahead: "In computers everything becomes smaller, faster, and cheaper. Every year, everything is multiplied by a factor of two. Three years ago there was no way to produce a magazine on a computer. Two years ago there was no way to do color separation on a computer. Now you can do both. The result is that, as things move towards the desktop and become easier for anyone to use, you find yourself supplanted by in-house people doing your job. I started off finding out what clients needed and fitting the software to their needs. Right now I've set up my business to ride on the wave of technology. I figure out what can be done with the computer and I get clients by showing them what can be done. We do the things they're not ready to do in-house."

At *RIFP* we made sure we had a whole page given over to questions and letters people sent to us. But we're finding this isn't enough, because people hate to write letters nowadays. Our solution will be, assuming we can afford it in a year's time, to set up a toll-free line for people to call if they have any iguana questions. It will be a twenty-four-hour line we'll answer personally during office hours. If the caller's question is interesting enough, we'll publish the question and answer in the letters page. We've also set aside a column to thank people for calling.

Only when you get to know your customers really well will you be able to predict what they want. You'll analyze their individual personalities, you'll know what things they cherish and what they reject. If you provide what they need before they know they need it, you'll do wonderfully. You won't actually ''sell'' them anything, they'll come to you and practically beg you to take their money. You're much better off than a retailer trying to do the same thing. If a store owner decides his customers want red sunglasses and they don't, then he's stuck with two hundred pairs of red sunglasses. If you decide your customers want wake-up calls and it turns out they don't, then you just don't make the calls.

INSPIRE TRUST

If people trust you, they'll want to do business with you. But you'll probably meet them for only an hour or two. How can you inspire trust that quickly? The worst way is to say, ''Trust me.'' The best way to gain trust is to care for people. If you care about people, you like them and you want to know about them. Most people automatically like people who like them. Absorb everything you can about them while you're talking. Find out what they're worried about, hear their complaints. The complaints don't need to be at all relevant to the job you're doing. If you're a good listener, they'll realize you care about them. They'll trust you and come back to you. Who knows? You may even be able to help them solve a problem, which will make you invaluable. This is a technique you'll practice every day. Every meeting has to be as full of enthusiasm as the first. As a successful marketing consultant told us, ''You gotta be a regular Mother Teresa in this business.''

BE UNIQUE

By this we mean you'll look for ways to be different. Not wacky, just different. You need to set yourself apart from other companies. You've started to do this by becoming a friend to your customers rather than their imperial ruler. Reverse the maxim ''Never underestimate the gullibility of the American public.'' This attitude is what got businesses into the state they're in now. Turn it around, and always remember you should ''never underes-

timate the sophistication of the American public.'' Joel Tucciarone of Zoetics says, ''Mass marketing is marketing on the
averages. What I'm talking about is marketing on the differences.
And the difference that matters . . . is a difference in relationship.''

Here are some examples of companies that have managed to
create a different relationship with their customers.

- Forms and Worms, the real estate forms company, has
  found that a sense of humor really helps. The company
  has made a basic service—providing forms—into a fun
  transaction by enclosing a small plastic worm in each box.
  The CEO, Ruth Lambert, says that customers write back
  if the worm is missing, or if it arrives maimed or with a
  squashed tail. Some customers value the worms as cat toys,
  while some even collect them, putting them on hooks
  above their desks. For something as potentially ''invisi-
  ble'' as a form, Forms and Worms has created real awareness of the product and a reason to buy from them. ''We
  do have three small competitors, and they generally gouge
  us on price,'' said Lambert. ''But I never said we were
  the cheapest, I said we were the best.''
- In Japan a company called High Sets publishes a clothes
  catalog aimed at female office workers. In order to make
  itself more accessible, High Sets has done a number of
  things. It publishes an annual magazine that contains po-
  etry, photographs, thoughts, and comments, all sent in by
  the customers. They take their customers to the opera and
  on vacation. They even have a château in France the customers can visit. Some people have actually been married
  there.
- Some companies market themselves by being exclusive.
  One insurance company, U.S.A.A. in San Antonio, sells
  policies only to current or former officers in the armed
  forces. ''At one time, all insurance providers were either
  local or regional,'' says U.S.A.A. spokesman John Walmsley. ''But when you're in the military, you move around a
  lot, and if you were transferred from Podunk to Springfield,
  you'd need to get new insurance. So, in 1922, a group of

officers formed an insurance cooperative so they could take their coverage with them wherever they went.'' He notes that the company does very little advertising; word of mouth is its primary source of new business. "Our customers feel a real sense of dedication from us,'' says Walmsley, "which results in loyalty from them.'' Another insurance company, Amica Insurance Company in Rhode Island, will insure you only if you're referred by another client. This creates a sense of exclusivity, and gives the referrer the pleasure of introducing his friend to a good deal.

USE DIRECT MAIL, NOT INDISCRIMINATE MAIL

One useful way of establishing and maintaining a relationship with your customers if you can't speak with them face-to-face is to correspond with them regularly. For instance, our accountants, Bauman and Krasnoff, send us regular information letters about tax changes. Even if we can't make heads or tails of the information, their sending it to us shows us they care and think we're intelligent enough to figure it all out. But direct mail like this has to be used carefully. Too often it should be called Indiscriminate Mail.

It's a big waste of money to just buy a mailing list for one thousand dollars and send information to people in the hope that some of them might want your service. A good response is considered somewhere between a measly 2 percent and 3 percent. Elysa Lazar, publisher of *Sales and Bargains Report,* the shopping newsletter, doesn't think much of it. "I think direct mail is a waste of time and money. Any newsletter that uses mailing lists probably shouldn't be a newsletter. The best publicity is free.''

If you're starting up and you have a definite idea of who your customers might be, write them a personal letter, announcing who you are and what you do. Make it as individualized as possible and enclose two business cards. Sign each letter in blue ink so they don't think it's a photocopy. Once you've been in business awhile, use the detailed mailing list of people who have used your service. Send a formal, private invitation to any special events you're having, and invite everyone to bring a guest. Stay in touch with these people throughout the year. Send them cards for holidays and events. One dentist we know makes sure to send birthday cards to all his patients, as well as cards for the spring and winter holidays, and reminders for them to come in for their annual checkup. It really doesn't take much effort since he already has all the information—including birthdays—in his data base. After he'd done this for a couple of years, his patients began looking at him as part of their extended family.

You'll need to use all these relationship-building tools as a 21st Century entrepreneur, because, in this increasingly sophisticated and competitive marketplace, if the customer can't tell you apart from other companies, then you're a dead duck. Consistently good service will mean you create a large, happy group of return customers, and that your reputation will spread. Then whenever they need your service, they'll come to you.

REFINING YOUR RELATIONSHIP SKILLS

There are two other techniques you need to master in order to become a benevolent ruler of your business empire—the art of creating the perfect first and final impressions.

FIRST IMPRESSIONS

You must make a great first impression on your clients. It's a sad fact that, after however many thousands of years we've been evolving, we still judge most of our relationships on the first meeting. Of course, in social situations this impression can be revised, for better or for worse. But in business you don't get a second chance.

Be constantly vigilant; you never know when you'll run into a potential client. Pay attention to the way you act around town. People are going to draw conclusions about your company from your behavior. If you lose your temper waiting in line at the supermarket, you can bet the last dollar of your working capital that you'll alienate a potential customer who witnesses your tantrum. But if people see you being charming and courteous around town, they'll know you're the kind of person they want to do business with. If you are a grouch, make an effort to change. You'll find people will say, "You know, since you've started that business, you've been a much happier person."

Many of your first meetings will be over the phone. In this case there are certain basic rules to follow. When the phone rings, answer, "Hello, John Smith here." (That's assuming, of course, your name is John Smith.) Use an even, cheerful tone: You don't want to sound like a receptionist, but you want to be more formal than you would on your home phone. Immediately write down the name of the person who's calling. Throughout the conversation make little notes to yourself. If you can't spell the caller's name, or miss it altogether, at the end of the call, just before you say, "Thank you for calling," check the spelling. If a call comes through on another line, apologize and say you're going to put someone else on hold and that you'll be right back. Don't do this more than once during a conversation—let your machine pick up other calls. If you have Call Waiting and you find you're frequently interrupted, shell out the money for another line—it's more annoying to the other person to hear those Call Waiting clicks than it is to be asked to hold for a second.

When you're calling someone, make sure you have everything you need in front of you. You can be sure that after fruitlessly trying to get through to a CEO for days, you'll get through when your notes are in the other room. Never do what someone did to us the other day. She called us up and said, "Oh, God, who did I call? Hang on, I've got it somewhere. Here it is. Could I speak to Melissa Morgan, please?" Also, don't assume married couples have the same last name. Anyone who calls us and asks for Mr. Morgan is immediately hung up on. If you use an answering service, make sure they have the same high standards.

Making a good first impression in person is even more complicated. Let's begin with the way you look. You can't do anything about the look of your face, but you can make sure you have clean, neat hair. (Same goes for your beard, if applicable.) Dress conservatively. Go wild with your tie or one piece of jewelry if you think it's appropriate. At the risk of sounding like your parents, let us remind you that the proof of your creativity will be your excellent work, not your outfit.

Before your client comes in, wipe your sweaty hand on your handkerchief so your first physical contact isn't too unpleasant for him or her. Come out from behind your desk and greet the client with a fairly firm handshake (let him do the macho hard bit if they want) and a smile, then a gesture for him to sit down, saying something along the lines of, "Mr. Big, great to see you, glad you could make it; have a seat." Remember what we wrote about inspiring trust—be a good listener and, if necessary, force yourself to care.

If you're hosting a meal at a restaurant, make sure you're the last one to leave. It gives the whole meeting a proper sense of closure. Traditional behavior really works and truly inspires confidence. Go and look at the tenets of whatever religion you were brought up in. Chances are they'll have some good tips on how to treat strangers as though they were family. If you follow them, you'll inspire trust and create business.

LAST IMPRESSIONS

You should have some way of contacting your customers after they've used your service. How you do this depends on your service. Many professionals follow up with a telephone call or a visit. Doctors always call after an operation to check on the patient and arrange an appointment. Other professionals should do this too: Lawyers and realtors should always meet their clients after a deal has closed. Not only does it give the transaction a sense of closure, but it reassures the client that she's spent her money wisely. For some services, sending out a stamped, self-addressed postcard may be enough. Put a numbered rating system on the back and leave plenty of room for customers to write comments.

Follow up fairly quickly. If a customer is dissatisfied, but you contact him and remedy the problem as soon as you're told about it, you'll prevent the customer from telling his friends what a poor job you did. Perhaps you'll even be able to turn a mistake into good word of mouth. People like to be able to talk about how quickly a problem was solved.

When talking to your customer, find a way to say how glad you are that he chose your company. Ask whether there's anything else you can do for him. But don't hustle for referrals: That will make you appear desperate.

Remember: You're not selling something that can be touched. A man who buys a watch can look at it every day and see that it's working well. A man who paid to have his groceries delivered is always going to be wondering whether he should have just gone shopping himself. Service customers can only rely on their fleeting experience of the service to evaluate it. That's why it's up to you to make sure that their experience is as pleasant, professional, and memorable as possible.

THE LEGAL STUFF COUNTS, TOO

There are another couple of areas in which you'll need to pay attention to your relationships with clients and customers, although they aren't directly involved in marketing: your contracts and your collections. Both deserve your attention.

CONTRACTS

Trust is what you build your business relationships on. Contracts are what you're going to build the finances of your business on. Even the best of friends should have a contract drawn up between them when they do business together. Contracts can take different forms. When you fill in a slip requesting a subscription to a magazine, you're part of a contract. When you buy a bus ticket, you're agreeing to a contract. It's essentially a promise that one party will do or provide something in exchange for something else from a second party. Certain professions don't put anything down on paper to begin with: Doctors, lawyers, and CPAs, among many others, just send bills. If you're in that kind of profession, so be it, but otherwise, put it in writing, and don't start work until they sign.

Never feel awkward when you ask customers to sign a contract, even if they seem insulted. If they say it's not necessary, you can trust them, blame someone else (your accountant, your silent partner, the IRS, your mother), and insist on getting the signature. Offer them your pen, twist their arms, but get their names down. Your standard contract is one of the things you'll talk to your lawyer about. Check with any trade associations you belong to: They may have some standard contracts you can use as a starting point. Your lawyer may decide that you merely need customers to sign the job estimates you give them. Similarly, ask your lawyer whether you should have new clients fill out a credit application and then check their credit when the job isn't going to be paid in cash.

Here's a (fictional) contract between a school and a teacher.

St. Saviour's School
25 Bath Street
Hollywood, Fla. 10034

CONTRACT BETWEEN ST. SAVIOUR'S SCHOOL
AND
JAMES CHIPS

It is hereby agreed between James Chips and St. Saviour's School that he is appointed to the faculty of the school for the school year ending June 30, 1993. This contract shall be considered valid as of July 1, 1992.

It is further agreed that Mr. Chips shall serve as ninth grade teacher and will perform his duties at such times and in a manner prescribed by the headmaster. These duties will include supervision of students and attendance at such meetings of the faculty as may be required by the headmaster.

In consideration of these services St. Saviour's School shall pay him a salary of seventy five thousand three hundred dollars ($75,300.00). It is agreed that this salary and any other forms of compensation will be treated as confidential by the undersigned.

It is understood and agreed that should Mr. Chips desire to sever his connnection with the school and set aside this contract, he shall have the right to do so upon giving one month's written notice; and in view of this privilege hereby granted, the school may claim the same right and privilege.

The renewal of this contract shall be taken up by the school by not later than April 1, 1993.

Headmaster's signature:
Teacher's signature:
Date:
Original: Employee
Duplicate: St. Saviour's Business Office

COLLECTIONS

Like contracts, the way you collect your money depends on the kind of business you run. You made this decision when you set your fees back in Chapter Ten. At the iguana newsletter, our subscribers pay the yearly fee up front. Some lawyers total up the hours they work for you each month and charge you accordingly. Freelance editors charge by the hour or job, usually depending on what's convenient for the employers. If you plan to be doing a long-term job for a new company, then it might be a good idea to ask for half up front with the rest on delivery, or to bill by the month. The extra paperwork will be compensated for by a regular cash flow.

The following pages contain two examples of bills. The first is from a lawyer, the second from an accountant.

CLARK KENT
Attorney-at-Law
123 Lois Lane
Los Angeles, CA 11234
(213) 987-6543

January 10, 1994

Arthur Finney
Tulip Street
Plano, TX 12534

For services rendered in December 1993:

Clark Kent
  Review documents; legal research;
  telephone conversations with A. Finney
    1.5 hours @ $200 $300.00

James Strummer, paralegal
  Review separation agreement;
  telephone conversations with A. Finney
  and client
    1 hour @ $50 $50.00

                                   $350.00

JONATHAN CARTER
Certified Public Accountant
666 Madison Avenue
New York, NY 10022
(212) 876-5432

January 28, 1994

Bert Marcos
123 4th Street
New York, NY 12345

For analysis on various dates
during January 1994 of proposed
split of marital assets and
preparation of schedules
reflecting asset split
  (6.5 hours @ $150/hour) $975

POLICING YOUR EMPIRE:
DEALING WITH PROBLEMS

Not every day will go smoothly, and even when a project is
going well, there are bound to be minor problems of some sort
that affect your relationships with your clients or customers. It
could be as simple as someone calling with a complaint: She
doesn't like this or that. But, like the Boy Scouts, you've got to
"be prepared." It's important to have a written complaints policy,
well-known to everyone who works with you.

The Body Shop is a chain of stores that sells ecologically sound
cleansing and beauty products, and it's doing very well. One of
the reasons is that the stores will take back anything you buy from
them, no questions asked. They do it matter-of-factly and quickly,
with a smile. You just go up to the cashier, who either makes the
exchange or gives you a store credit right then and there. There's
none of the "you should be receiving a check sometime in the
next six months" that Bloomingdale's gives you, assuming
you've found the well-hidden returns counter.

The Body Shop is dealing with problems in a 21st Century
way. Bloomingdale's is dealing with them in a nineteenth-century
way. Make sure you react quickly. Keep a complaints log and
write down everything that's criticized and how you fixed it. If
you see a pattern of complaints emerging, then isolate the problem
and solve it quickly. It's a good idea to send a letter of apology
to customers after you've solved the problem. You don't need to
grovel, just be sincere.

There are three more serious problems that could arise. You
fail to complete the job, your client fails to pay you, or you're
struck down by the Mighty Hand of Fate.

WHEN YOU CAN'T PRODUCE

Let's say something has gone wrong with your end of the deal
and you haven't produced what was asked for in the contract.
This could happen for many reasons, but basically, it's either your
fault or it's not. If it is your fault, you must apologize and offer

to make it up to the client in any way possible. There's no way around it. Give a simple explanation of the facts if it's requested; otherwise just tell the client you'll find a way to complete the job quickly and do it for free. The client may never come back to you, but at least he won't be able to say you just ran away.

If the mistake wasn't your fault, you still need to do all the preceding. But this time you get to let your aggression out on whoever screwed up. If it's someone in your office, you'll need to tread carefully, but be firm. We discuss this more in the next chapter. If it's a free-lancer, feel free to use all the techniques you ever learned from every dysfunctional family you ever knew: Intimidation, aggression, guilt, and shouting are good for a start. Make sure the person responsible for the mistakes does the right job for free and, if possible, apologizes to your client.

WHEN YOUR CLIENT TRIES TO FREELOAD

Even worse than the preceding scenario is the possibility of the client not coughing up the money. What do you do if a check has been in the mail for thirty days? You have two choices. You can let it go and bad-mouth the client around town or you can go to court. Your local small-claims court is the place to do this. But ask your lawyer how much it's going to cost you first. The best way to avoid being stiffed completely is to have a good contract. If you don't like the look of a customer (see, those first impressions really do count) or have heard bad things, then insist on a half-now, half-on-delivery deal. Just be wary. Don't become completely reliant on one customer. If he or she drops you or goes bust, you'll be out of business too.

"As the economy began to get worse," says Anna Walker, the illustrator, "I found I was being paid slower and slower. You just need to constantly remember that it's not personal, so don't be embarrassed; just call up and ask for the money calmly. If you've got any hang-ups about money, leave them at the door: People are just weird about money." Walker had a bad experience when she tried to collect payment after doing some work for two people who were free-lancers themselves. "Well, they suddenly decided they'd fallen in love. So they ran off together to Santa Fe, leaving no word of their whereabouts, having taken my artwork already and owing me twenty-five hundred dollars. It took a while, but after I contacted the company directly, I eventually got my money.''

WHEN FATE STEPS IN

As Anita Loos so precisely put it, ''Fate keeps on happening.'' What do you do if fate happens to your business deal? Say, for example, the county fair you organized is washed away when the Mississippi breaks its banks, or Mitzi the poodle has a heart attack when you take out the dog-styling shears. Well, you can insure, you can pray, or you can hope for the best. We recommend a combination of the last two methods. Anyway, most insurance policies don't cover ''acts of God,'' like floods, insurrections, revolutions, and earthquakes. On the other hand, reexamining our policy, we're comforted to see we're covered for fire resulting from nuclear action.

HOW TO DEAL WITH SUCCESS IN THE 21ST CENTURY

Make sure you're ready to handle the crowds your marketing will attract. You'll have a loyal, ever-growing population eager to do business with you. You must grow at a steady pace or you'll find yourself unable to give everyone the quality service that attracted them in the first place. If that happens, you'll lose customers. The solution is to appear to be exclusive. It's better to be thought of as exclusive than to risk spreading yourself thin. A lost customer is harder to woo back than someone who hasn't used your service at all. If you reach the point of having to turn people away, you just say, ''I'm sorry, but I really wouldn't be able to do you or my present clients justice if I took on a new customer. I'm going to be expanding my business during the next two months, and if you still need someone to help you then, well, I'd be more than happy to see what I could do.'' (Meanwhile, run around like crazy, get refinanced, and expand. We'll discuss this in Chapters Sixteen and Seventeen.)

As a service business in the vanguard of this new empire of "Friendship in Business," you should be proud of yourself and confident you can succeed. You're small, flexible, and willing to listen. You're exactly what 21st Century consumers want. You're someone they can trust.

For more information on the topics covered in Chapters Twelve and Thirteen, take a look at the following books:

- *Big Ideas for Small Businesses: How to Successfully Advertise, Publicize, & Maximize Your Business or Professional Practice,* by Marilyn and Tom Ross (Comm Creat, 1993)
- *Do-It-Yourself Direct Marketing: Secrets for Small Business,* by Mark S. Bacon (Wiley, 1991)
- *Great Ad!: Do-It-Yourself Advertising for Your Small Business,* by Carol Wallace (TAB, 1990)
- *Guerilla P.R.: How to Wage an Effective Publicity Campaign—Without Going Broke,* by Michael Levine (Harper, 1993)
- *How to Advertise: A Handbook for the Small Business,* by Sandra L. Dean (Dearborn, 1983)
- *How to Promote Your Business,* by John Hathaway-Bates (Nerthus, 1981)
- *Marketing Ideas for Small Service Businesses* (Gordon, 1992)
- *Power Marketing for Small Business,* by Jody Horner (Oasis, 1993)
- *Producing Your Own Brochure-Catalog,* by Alan Smith (Success, 1990)
- *You Can Spend Less & Sell More: The Advertising Book,* by William K. Witcher (Mark, 1988)

COACH YOUR TEAM TO VICTORY

You and the People Who Work for You

Opening day is approaching quickly, and almost everything is in place. There's really only one last part of the plan that you need to pull together: your employees. Don't skip this chapter, even if you think it's irrelevant to your one-person business. One person start-ups have a habit of growing. So that you can respond confidently and accurately to this potential expansion, you must plan ahead and determine how you want your company to grow.

Some companies need employees just to get going; others need them to increase efficiency; still others need them in order to expand. We'll explore these needs, while discussing the best ways to hire people to work for you, and how to get the most out of them. Up until now we've been describing the 21st Century entrepreneur as a determined individual who can get things done alone. However, eventually you'll need to rely on other people, whether you stay a solo operator and hire free-lancers or consultants, or you decide to put other workers on your payroll. In either case, you'll be the boss. We suggest, though, instead of thinking of yourself as the boss, think of yourself as a coach, with all the commitment to excellence, understanding, and ability to inspire that role requires.

WHAT MAKES A GOOD COACH?

Think back to the coaches at your school. What did you like about them? What did you dislike? While researching this chapter we suddenly found ourselves full of sympathy for the men and women who tried to whip our puny adolescent bodies into something resembling a winning team. When we were in high school, one of the things we disliked most about coaches was that we felt they didn't give everyone a chance. Obviously not everyone could make the team, but after a while certain people (us) stopped trying out and basically just gave up organized sports. Now, looking back on this selection process, it doesn't seem as unfair as it did then. There were tryouts every season, and if we'd practiced every night during the three months prior, maybe we'd have made the team. And let's face it, the coach wanted a winning team, and so the best players were going to be picked. You're in the coach's position now and you're going to find it hard to pick your team.

What we liked best about some of our coaches was their perpetual optimism and ability to inspire. Who knows what they were like at home or in the faculty room? In front of their students they held their heads high and were certain that this was the game that would turn around that nine-game losing streak. This ability to inspire will be crucial to your success. Confidence rubs off easily on others, and you'll find yourself trying to encourage everyone in your business.

Another trait we liked about the best coaches was that, although they had to pick the best players for their teams, they didn't ignore the other students in regular gym class. They saw when students were trying hard and praised them for it. They also told you straight out when you did something stupid. The best coaches also knew that everyone needed individual attention and that we were all inspired by different things. Some people respond best to direct orders, others like to be teased along, while some are best left to do their own thing. Good coaches can shift their personality from a domineering drill sergeant to a let-it-all-hang-out hippie.

Here are three key points that will help you become a good coach to your employees.

YOUR ATTITUDE

If you think about the jobs you've done and try to pick out your favorite, we think you'll find it was the job in which you had the most fun, not the job that paid best. Money can make up for a lot, but it can't keep you in a job that you loathe, especially one in which you're working for an unsympathetic boss. As a boss, you aren't going to be able to pay as well as some bigger companies, so you'll need to compensate your workers in other ways. For a start, you need to be understanding. Listen to their problems. Don't accept every excuse, whether for sloppiness or tardiness, but at least hear them out and give them the benefit of the doubt if possible. Be grateful to people if they do what you want them to do, when you want them to do it. Most important, you should definitely develop a sense of irony and humor. It'll keep everyone sane.

MONEY

However charming you are and however pleasant you are to be around, you won't get people to do anything for you unless you pay them what you owe them, on time. Choose one day of the week as payday and make sure your employees get paid on that day. It's okay for you to put off paying your own salary until a major supplier pays its bill, but don't ask anyone else to wait. When free-lancers hand over the finished product, if possible, hand them back a check.

PRECISION AND CLARITY

Tell people exactly what you want and when you want it, while respecting the fact that people often need to give things their own twist. Bear in mind that some people think asking questions makes them look stupid, so they hesitate to ask for needed clarification. Do everything you can to make sure your directions are as specific and clear as they can be. Then give people as much time as you can, but insist they finish the work by the deadline.

WHY DO YOU EVEN NEED A TEAM?

It's obvious that you can't do everything on your own, and that you at least need to hire experts like your CPA and your lawyer. It may also be the nature of your business that you need outside help to provide your service. To get the work out, you may choose to rely on a network of free-lancers, or you may hire employees in your office; for instance, someone who answers the telephone and makes appointments or someone who does artwork for you.

At *RIFP* we knew that although we would do most of the writing ourselves, from time to time there were going to be things that we couldn't do. The first such problem was when we had to come up with a logo. We tried taking photos of Iggy and Squiggy and drawing from that, but they always came out looking like basset hounds. We asked around and found a couple of free-lance artists. We interviewed them, looked at their portfolios, and picked one of them to design our logo. The design she came up with was clear, simple, and eye-catching—just what we wanted. Now we go back to her every time we need some sort of graphics done.

Another problem we had was the large amount of mail that came in every day. We solved this problem by hiring a friend of ours as a free-lance mail opener. Whenever we get too many letters to deal with, she comes by and sorts it all out. Another occasional team member is a graduate student at the nearby university. We ask him to do research for us in the library when we need to tackle a particularly difficult reptile question.

HOW ARE YOU GOING TO HIRE YOUR TEAM?

Legally, you've two choices about the way you're going to hire your workers. Either you'll make them employees, or they'll be autonomous and be considered independent contractors or free-lancers. As you'll see, there are advantages and disadvantages to both.

EMPLOYEES

Relations between employer and employee have changed since the 1950s. No longer does an employee sign on for life, and no longer does the employer expect to look after all the employee's needs. The relationship is much more distant: Both sides silently recognize it won't last forever. The employer is still in charge, but he or she must earn respect, rather than obedience.

The disadvantages of hiring workers as employees rather than as independent contractors are many. For a start, all the taxes and forms you fill out for yourself, you'll also need to do for your employees. Here's a partial list of the tax and government obligations you'll take on: Social Security taxes need to be withheld from your employees' paychecks and matched by you; federal income taxes need to be withheld; state and city income taxes need to be withheld; you need to organize worker's compensation insurance in case of injury on the job; and you need to contribute to state unemployment insurance, which involves a lot of paperwork and money.

Hiring an employee may even limit your company's growth: Besides dealing with all the extra costs and paperwork, you're bound to lose some of the flexibility you had with a one-person business. If you hire an employee, you'll probably need to rent an office rather than work from your home. Neighbors expect you to be coming in and out all day, and may overlook the fact that you're running a business from your home, but they might object to another person being there all the time. It makes the office seem more of an office. Besides, do you want someone else in your home eight hours a day?

If you want to attract good people, you'll also need to offer some fringe benefits. Some of these benefits are regarded almost as basic rights nowadays; for example, paid vacations, health insurance, and a pension plan. By the time you total up all the extra costs, you can basically add another third to the salaries you'll be paying.

Health insurance is often the only reason people choose to stay with a large company rather than start their own businesses or go to work for a small outfit like yours. While the details of Clinton's health plan will be debated right up until it's enacted, health insurance is, in effect, already mandatory: You'd be hard-pressed to find someone willing to work for you who didn't want some sort of medical coverage. It's especially important for older employees and single parents who find the cost of buying health insurance directly from a carrier prohibitive. You can definitely attract good employees if you have a good health policy. It's up to you to decide whether it's worth the extra three hundred to four hundred dollars a month it will cost you.

If your employees are part-time, they're likely to be older people, students, or mothers. For students and mothers, some control over their hours is essential. You'll need to see whether you can accommodate their schedules. If you can, then do so: Trying to coordinate child care or school can be a nightmare, and they're likely to reward you with loyalty and hard work if you make their lives easier to organize.

After all that, there are a few advantages to having full-time employees. It frees you up to do the things you want to do. Instead of answering the phone or keeping the books or chasing down unpaid bills, you can get on with the part of the business that you like. You might even be able to go on vacation! Other companies may take you more seriously if you have another employee. It certainly helps to have someone else answer the phone. To the caller, a receptionist or secretary conjures up a large office and a waiting room. And if you don't want to talk to someone, you can be in a meeting.

If you decide to go this route, make sure you have a good employment contract that takes into account the laws in your state. You need to be especially careful about "terminating" or firing people. It's easier than ever for disgruntled employees to find reasons to sue you. While this is a big step forward for workers, you must be very careful in your hirings and firings.

If you've planned for an employee in your business checklist, if you're convinced that the extra efficiency will pay the extra salary, if you can afford to offer good fringe benefits as well as a decent wage, and if you're a good boss, you'll find that you can probably get, and keep, loyal, enthusiastic employees. The best that could happen is that you all grow together with the business. The worst that can happen is that the added burden of an employee puts you out of business.

FREE-LANCERS

The disadvantage of hiring free-lancers, or independent contractors, is that you need to trust that other people can do what
you want them to do, without being under your direct supervision.
Most of the time it's a good idea to trust others. But when the
success of a project depends on a missing piece of artwork or
copy that you gave to someone else to work on, trust seems less
attractive. Basically, you need to be dependent on other people's
professionalism. That's why it's important to interview independent contractors the way you would any other employee. We'll
show you how to do this later in the chapter.

There are a lot of advantages, however. Essentially, hiring free-
lancers allows you to expand (and contract) as needed. There's
no paperwork to speak of, you save money on all the insurance
and health care costs, and you can still work from home. Of
course, you need to pay your free-lancers a higher salary than
you would an employee, because they need to pay their own taxes
and health care costs. But take some solace from the fact that
you're also helping to build a network of people like yourself,
21st Century entrepreneurs.

Frequently you'll find that you form temporary partnerships
with other businesses. Your firm may be one of three or four hired
by a larger company to execute a project. At the first meeting
there may be five people in the conference room, three of them
entrepreneurs like yourself, the fourth a businessman coordinating
everyone's efforts. For the duration of the project you will all
work together, and when it's over, you'll go your separate ways.
However, if you're pleased with your teammates' work, you'll
know who to contact if you have a similar project in the future.
In the 21st Century such strategic alliances will offer you a way to
expand and contract as business needs dictate. You'll stay flexible.

The only thing you need to watch out for is the legal status of
your independent contractors. If they become too dependent on
you, the IRS may consider them your employees, in which case
you'll be liable for all the taxes and insurance you hoped to escape.
Accountant Stuart Bauman says this about independent contractor

law: "Recently the IRS and the Department of Labor have been cracking down on this area aggressively. The biggest question you need to ask yourself is, is the person doing the work for you under your direct authority? If you're there, telling someone what to do on the job, if you're guiding the worker through the process, even over the phone, then it's an employee/employer relationship. But if he or she has a business of his or her own and other customers, then you'll be okay." The IRS and the DOL have different concerns. "The big deal with the DOL," according to Bauman, "is employee insurance. They look to see whether the worker has any insurance, like worker's compensation. If none is there, the DOL may come looking for it from you. Sometimes the IRS will get wind of it and come after you for the Social Security taxes and the rest of it."

There are some safeguards you can take. Bauman suggests making sure that you verify that people you employ as independent contractors have their own letterhead paper and business cards, and that other people are employing them too. When you pay them, do it in response to bills they send you, and keep the bills. Making the payments every month rather than every week also makes the checks seem less like a wage. Although you need to watch this part of the law carefully, we feel that hiring outside help is definitely the best for a small service business. The precautions you need to take are much easier than dealing with all the government's paperwork for employees.

HOW DO YOU FIND THE BEST TEAM?

Finding your workers has never been easy. Here are some hints on putting together your team.

FINDING GREAT EMPLOYEES

Up until now you've probably been the person applying for jobs. It's a whole different experience when you're on the other side of the desk. Find your pool of applicants by first using personal contacts and then by putting an advertisement in the newspaper and checking with employment agencies. Ask for a résumé. Hiring relatives might seem like a cheap way to find help, but it's probably not a good idea. Your sister still needs to be paid something, and let's face it, you're not going to be able to give her a tough talk about trying harder when you know you'll be seeing her at your mother's this weekend.

Once you have a decent number of responses, sit down and pick the best applicants. Call them up and schedule appointments, then pick up some application forms at a stationery store. During the interviews pay attention to the way they act, as well as the things they say. They are supposed to be on their best behavior in front of you. If they can't keep their fingers out of their noses now, they'll probably be even worse in the office. If they have samples of the work they've done, look at them carefully and listen to their explanations. They should be confident and proud of their work. When they've left, try to make a snap decision: Could you work with them? Write down your thoughts so you can refer back to them. Later on, you should follow up on the references they've given you. Be thorough and check that what they've told you is correct. A good question to ask previous employers is whether they would rehire your applicants if the chance came up.

You will be looking for the following abilities when you screen applicants: Can they solve problems? Do they have pleasing personalities? Do they have a knowledge of your field? This last quality may or may not be crucial. You may be looking for someone who can add to your knowledge, or you may want someone who is willing to learn from you.

However much experience the candidate has had, having an ability to analyze and solve problems is critically important. How you test for this during the interview depends on the sort of business you're running. A good way to assess a person's ability to think quickly is to ask the applicant what he or she would do in a certain situation. For example, how would the interviewee deal with a disgruntled client? What would she do if she realized she wasn't going to be able to finish a project for you on time?

Naturally, an appealing personality is extremely important in a service business. How does the interviewee strike you? Do you like and trust him or her? Imagine you're a customer meeting this person. Would he or she inspire trust? Don't settle for second best or "maybe." If you aren't sure, advertise again. Your business's success may depend on the quality of your staff.

When you've found the person you want, call and schedule another interview during which you can explain the philosophy of the business in a little more detail and talk about where you want the business to go. Explain that there will be a trial period of ninety days (or whatever seems appropriate to you) and then offer the job.

One last word: Give your new employee a chance. We're all entitled to make a few mistakes. But be honest with yourself if it doesn't work out. Don't keep someone on out of pity.

FINDING GREAT FREE-LANCERS

Hiring free-lancers is a similar process, but there are a few important differences. For a start, you're far more likely to rely on personal or professional contacts than advertising to find the people you want to hire. Your interview with the free-lancer is likely to be more of a meeting of equals than it was when you were looking for employees. In fact, you yourself may be a free-lancer looking for someone you can subcontract out to. As we've said, it's important that your free-lancers have an economic life beyond the work you're offering them so that you won't be any one person's sole source of income. This way you'll avoid any problems with the IRS and the concept of independent contractors. Look carefully at free-lancers' portfolios or any other samples of their work. If you decide to go with one person, explain exactly what you need and when you need it by. Describe what you're trying to do at your company and promise more work if you like the results of this assignment. Only hire people you'd feel comfortable firing. It's never easy to fire someone, but it's even harder if he or she's a friend. As with regular employees, you can't afford to keep someone on out of pity. If you aren't sure about someone, wait until you have a small job to use as a test. Change free-lancers every now and again just to see who else is out there and to show the IRS that these are really free-lancers.

The good news for you is that free-lancers don't want to get too involved with you either. And seeing as you're going to be paying them, they're willing to put up with a lot. "You don't need to be pals with the people offering you work," says free-lance illustrator Anna Walker. "The qualities you're looking for in someone who's going to employ you are not what you look for in a friend. You just want someone with lots of money, and the good taste to hire you!"

Now you know how to go about getting your team together and how to make it a winning one. It may be more of a loose alliance than a team, but you're their coach, and you can bring out the best in your players. You're ready to open for business. In the next chapter we'll show you how to handle all the money that we hope will be coming in.

For more information on the topics covered in Chapter Fourteen, take a look at the following books:

- *A Small Business Guide To Employee Selection,* by Lynn Grensing (ISC, 1986)
- *Employee Benefits for Small Business,* by Jane White (Prentice-Hall, 1991)
- *Fringe Benefits Guidebook for Small Businesses,* by Steven A. Hopfenmuller (Hooksett, 1987)
- *Guide To Small Business Consulting Engagements,* by Douglas R. Carmichael, William J. Gole, Don Pallais, and Herbert S. Schecter (Pretner, 1991)
- *Human Relations in Small Business,* by Elwood Chapman (Crisp, 1993)
- *Small Business Subcontracting Directory* (Gordon, 1990)
- *Starting a Small Business: Hiring, Compensating & Evaluating,* by Robert E. and Anita E. Worthington (Oasis, 1987)

III.

THE BIG LEAP

You've been planning carefully for months now. You're starting to do your marketing. You know how much money you need to make in order to survive, and you know precisely how you're going to make it. There's nothing left to do except open for business!

We can't push you over the edge. We can, and have, taken you by the hand to the precipice. And we will go on to help those who make the jump in the remaining chapters of this book. But we can't take the risk for you. There is no guarantee. You've prepared better than anyone else in the world could for this moment. If you're an entrepreneur at heart, we'll see you on the other side of the gorge that separates entrepreneurs from the rest of the populace. If you're not there, maybe we'll see you sometime in the future when your confidence is higher. Anyway, good luck . . .

Welcome to those of you who have made the jump. The first thing to do now is celebrate. Have an opening party, or do a special promotion, or whatever you think would be appropriate. Rent a restaurant if you don't want to have people standing around your tiny desk in your apartment! Invite your backers and any clients you may already have. Spend a little money on some good food and fresh flowers. This is your chance to make a good first impression with potential customers.

The next day you must settle down and conduct business as usual. Sound as confident as someone who's been in operation for two years and has a flourishing business. You can't afford to let your fear show: No one will trust you if you're nervous.

If you don't have any customers in the first week, you should reexamine your marketing. Your market research showed there were customers out there; you just need to find them. If people are interested in your service but don't hire you, then find out what it is they're looking for or what it is they thought you were offering. You may need to reposition your business slightly to appeal to them. Listen to what the customers want, even if it wasn't exactly what you were planning to offer.

If you get off to a flying start, make sure you keep detailed, scrupulous records of everything that goes on, so that you can analyze exactly how you're making your money.

There's really nothing to it; just go ahead, do business, and have fun. It's not going to be smooth sailing—but then, what in life is? There are some important decisions you'll need to make once your company is thriving. The last three chapters will help you make these choices so you can continue to prosper.

❧ 15 ❧
YOU AND YOUR YO-YO

Day-to-Day Finances

It would be great if businesses were like toy trains and you could simply lay out the track, wind them up, and watch them go. Unfortunately, a business is more like a yo-yo. You must be careful how you wind the string around your yo-yo, you must release it carefully, and once it's in motion, you must keep a constant eye on it. Getting your yo-yo running is no mean feat—and neither is running a business. Fortunately, in both cases it's actually fun, and you're personally involved enough to make it work.

You must make constant adjustments in order to improve your business's financial health. You'll know what adjustments to make by using some basic accounting techniques. Now, we're sure you think you're paying your accountant quite enough and he should be doing this work, but you really do have an obligation to your company. You must get involved and understand just how well or badly you're doing. And in the long run, it'll also save you money.

The key to success in record keeping and accounting is to keep things as simple as possible. There's no point in accounting for its own sake. The only reason to do it is to get a more accurate picture of how successfully your business is doing. You'll want to be able to compare your past and present performances from week to week, as well as month to month. You need to have a firm grasp of your cash flow so you'll be able to predict how your business is going to grow.

We'll show you some useful techniques that can give you different pictures of your business: the profit and loss statement, the

203

balance sheet, and business ratios. Rather like snapshots of you playing with a yo-yo, they're useful as illustrations of frozen moments, but ultimately aren't complete pictures of your business. Individually, their usefulness is limited; taken together, they may provide a useful portrait and should give you some hints on what to be wary of. They give you an indication of what you're doing right or wrong, and to an extent, they can predict your future.

Your basic tool is a bookkeeping system. The simplest, called the cash method, is just like using a checkbook. (You can make up a ledger for yourself or buy one from a stationery store.) There are other ways of bookkeeping, such as the single-entry system and the double-entry system, which use either the cash or accrual methods. Ask your accountant to explain these terms and figure out which would be best for you. But try to use the method that's simplest for you. If keeping your receipts in a paper bag and adding them up on the back of the *TV Guide* works for you, then that's all you need to do. If you need to learn double-entry bookkeeping with the accrual method, then go ahead and learn it. Look at computer programs like Quicken or Excel. These can really speed up calculation and projection. Talk it over with your accountant. He'll probably advise you—wisely—to use something more than a paper bag and less than the full-blown double-entry system. If he has any sense, he'll also make sure you know about some of the following.

You already did a simple break-even projection in Chapter Ten when you were figuring out how much working capital you needed and what price you'd charge. You also know what volume of sales you must achieve by what time in order to break even. For our newsletter we decided we needed to sell 156 subscriptions within a year at seventy-five dollars each in order to break even. Now you can go into slightly more complex calculations. We'll show you how to figure out whether your money is moving through the business sensibly. You'll also learn how much money you've made so far. We'll show you how to approximate what your business is worth and what this figure can tell you about the health of your business. Finally we'll examine what to do if your economic string gets knotted and your precious yo-yo of a business seems to be heading out of control.

IS YOUR MONEY MOVING SMOOTHLY?—THE PROFIT AND LOSS STATEMENT

Analyzing the flow of money through the year keeps you on top of your finances at all times. In Chapter Ten you tried to predict what you'd earn. Cash-flow analysis with a month-by-month profit-and-loss statement keeps track of what actually happens every month. You should know when a big bill is going to be due and you should have enough money available to pay it. If the cash isn't there, you'll be stuck. There's nothing more frustrating than owning a growing, generally successful business that's completely stalled because you can't pay a bill you should have known was coming. The only thing that's worse is when someone else owes you the missing money. You're helpless, frustrated, and possibly out of business. These cash-flow problems are two of the most common reasons given for small business failure. The sad thing is that usually they occur because the owner failed to plan ahead and monitor the cash flow every week and every month.

The good news is, service businesses usually do well as far as cash flow goes. There are variations, of course: For example, a window washer gets paid faster than a lawyer, but they are both better off than a storekeeper. Owners of retail businesses may be forced to wait a long time before they collect any money on goods they've bought. They also have the problem of storing unsold inventory. Remember, with service businesses the inventory is more elusive. On the one hand, you can bill someone as soon as he or she leaves your office, and your inventory won't become obsolete; on the other, if no one hires you all day, you can't take that time and add it onto the next work day—the day's "inventory" is lost for good.

You already tried to estimate your monthly income when you did your break-even projection in Chapter Ten. After a few months of actual business, you can revise these estimates with real numbers, for better or worse. Even if you appear to be doing well, you must take time to look at the longer trends: You need to know what is going to happen, as well as what has happened. As you can imagine, this is the sort of thing a computer is useful for. Have your accountant recommend a good program. We provide a blank profit-and-loss statement for you in Appendix D.

Here's our profit-and-loss statement for the first year's operation of *RIFP:*

Month-by-Month Profit-and-Loss Statement for *Raising Iguanas for Fun and Profit*

	Jan	Feb	March
Number of subscriptions sold at $75:	6	9	12
Sales revenue:	$450	$675	$900
Cash inflow from subscriptions:	$0	$450	$675
Less costs:[1]	$474	$474	$474
Net income before taxes:	($474)	($24)	($201)

	April	May	June
Number of subscriptions sold at $75:	7	11	5
Sales revenue:	$525	$825	$375
Cash inflow from subscriptions:	$900	$525	$825
Less costs:	$474	$474	$474
Net income before taxes:	$426	$51	$351

	July	Aug	Sept
Number of subscriptions sold at $75:	8	17	21
Sales revenue:	$600	$1,275	$1,575

[1] You'll notice our costs remain the same every month. This is because, as we explained in Chapter Ten, we aren't yet doing enough business for our postage or printing costs to rise.

	July	Aug	Sept
Cash inflow from subscriptions:	$375	$600	$1,275
Less costs:	$474	$474	$474
Net income before taxes:	($99)	$126	$801

	Oct	Nov	Dec
Number of subscriptions sold at $75:	14	27	19
Sales revenue:	$1,050	$2,025	$1,425
Cash inflow from subscriptions:	$1,575	$1,050	$2,025
Less costs:	$474	$474	$474
Net income before taxes:	$1,101	$576	$1,551

Having this information allowed us to do a number of things. For a start, we were able to work out whether or not we'd made a profit for the year. It also let us see how our cash flow was doing throughout the year.

First Year's Income Statement

Number of subscriptions sold at $75:	156
Sales revenue:	$11,700
Cash inflow:	$10,275
(missing $1,425, which will arrive in Jan. for Dec.'s subs)	
Less costs:	$5,688
Net income before taxes:	$4,587

As you can see, everything depended on actually selling our subscriptions. If we had gone as far as August and had sold only forty subscriptions, then we would have known we had a problem—we could never sell 116 subscriptions in four months. (Later in this chapter we'll discuss what to do if you realize that you're in this situation.) At the end of each quarter and at the end of the year you and your accountant should prepare a profit-and-loss statement based on the figures you've gathered, and then compare it with your plan to see whether you're on track.

Keeping track of and analyzing your cash flow isn't excessively complicated, but it is crucial. If we'd been judging our success by the amount of money coming in, we might have thought we were doing well in June. Look back at the profit-and-loss statement and you'll see that things for that month seemed fine. We'd received checks for $825 and our net income was firmly positive, when only the month before, we'd just scraped by with $51. The truth was more complicated, however. Because we'd managed to sell only five subscriptions in June, by July we were actually doing terribly: A few more months of that and we'd be out of business. So it was fortunate that in August, PBS aired a special show about the sex life of the iguana. This stirred a great deal of interest in our reptiles and boosted sales for the next month.

The cardinal rule of cash flow is that cash is king: Collect your money early. If someone won't pay up, the best thing is to get on the telephone immediately. Tell the company you need the money; convince them you're the creditor they owe it to the most. The more noise you make, the more likely it is you'll get results. If you have a penalty clause in your contract for late payment, then this is the time to mention it, but sweeten the threat by reminding them that next time, if they pay early, there's a $\frac{1}{2}$ percent discount. After the telephone call, send a polite but firm letter repeating what you've said. Unless you're trying to collect a huge bill, using a collection agency probably isn't worth it because they'll take about a third of whatever they get for you.

HOW MUCH IS YOUR BUSINESS WORTH?—THE BALANCE SHEET

The simple answer is, probably not a lot to anyone but you. Because you are so much of the business and you are, as far as finances go, an intangible asset, there wouldn't be much business left if you weren't involved. Nevertheless, banks, CPAs, and the IRS like to know how much you're worth from time to time, so you've got to work it out. As we'll see, it also gives you some information about your business's health. What we're doing is drawing up a balance sheet, because your assets are supposed to be performing a sort of balancing act with your debts. Of course, you hope the scale tips down on the side of your debts. Your accountant will organize the comprehensive statements for the

IRS and the banks, but you should also be able to work out an informal version for yourself. Let's work out what *RIFP* was worth in December.

Balance sheet for
Raising Iguanas for Fun and Profit
for December 31

ASSETS
<u>Current assets</u>

Cash	$2,025	
Accounts receivable	$1,425	
Inventories	<u>$0</u>	
Total current assets		$3,450
<u>Fixed assets</u>		
Office equipment	<u>$3,140</u>	
Total fixed assets		<u>$3,140</u>
TOTAL ASSETS		<u>$6,590</u>
LIABILITIES		
Current liabilities	$0	
Accounts payable	$474	
Reserve for taxes	$1,000	
Surplus	<u>$5,116</u>	
TOTAL LIABILITIES		<u>$6,590</u>

By putting in the surplus, we are able to make the balance actually balance. The surplus isn't all readily available profit: It includes our office equipment and the $1,425 we'll be receiving in January for the subscriptions we sold in December. We'd be more shortsighted than Iggy and Squiggy, our darling iguanas, if we were to think our business was actually worth the surplus line in the liabilities section above. And we'd be insane to think anyone would buy the business from us.

However, we do now know we're not way off track. We don't have a lot of money owed to us (accounts receivable) and we don't owe a lot to anyone (current liabilities). If our balance sheet showed that our liabilities were much bigger than our assets, we'd know we were going to need to do a lot of fine-tuning. The only thing to do is to stop, analyze what went wrong, and decide whether we want to try again.

Now that we know what our assets and liabilities are, we can look at the relationship between the two numbers. Our assets at the newsletter were $6,590, and our liabilities (excluding the surplus) were $1,474. Put as a ratio, x:y, that makes $6,590:$1,474, or almost 4.5:1. A ratio of 2:1 is considered safe, so we were doing very well. If something went wrong, we would even have enough financial leeway to correct the mistake before it became catastrophic. If we owed our relatives a lot of money and they were demanding it back—in other words, if we had a lot of debt—then we'd want to keep the ratio about 3:1. On the other hand, once we knew we were doing pretty well, we could let the ratio slip as low as 1.5:1 should we need to use some working capital for a special promotion.

At *RIFP* we run a fairly simple operation. What follows is a balance sheet for a more complicated business. Robert Somerset runs a company called Byte-24 that rents computers. There's a blank version of this for you to use in Appendix E.

**Balance sheet for
Byte-24
for December 31**

ASSETS
<u>Current assets</u>

Cash on hand	$732	
Cash in bank	$5,324	
Accounts receivable	$2,056	
Merchandise inventory	$8,234	
Supplies	$698	
Prepaid rent	$2,800	
Total current assets		$19,844
<u>Fixed assets</u>		
Office equipment	$14,540	
Less accumulated depreciation	$2,000	
Total fixed assets		$12,540
TOTAL ASSETS		$32,384

LIABILITIES
<u>Current liabilities</u>

Accounts payable	$5,804	

Note payable to bank	$850	
Income taxes payable	$2,300	
Total current liabilities		$8,954
Owner's equity		
Robert Somerset, capital on January 1	$17,785	
Plus net income for year	$10,145	
Minus withdrawals by owner	$4,500	
Robert Somerset, capital on December 31		$23,430
TOTAL LIABILITIES		$32,384

Although the end result is the same as *RIFP*'s simpler balance sheet—the books balance and all the money is accounted for—there are some terms here that should be explained. *Cash on hand* means the money Robert Somerset has in his cash register at the shop. The rest of his cash is in the bank earning interest. *Merchandise inventory* is how much he paid for the unsold paper, computer disks, and software that he sells as a sideline. The cost of any unused miscellaneous stuff used around the shop—like stationery, cleaning liquid, or garbage bags—comes under the heading *supplies*. Somerset's accountant has determined that his computers will depreciate in value by around $2,000, so that amount is reduced from his assets. The accountant also told him to put some money aside to pay taxes, so you can see there is $2,300 listed in the liability section for that purpose. The equity section is where the really important information lies. By comparing what his business was worth on January 1 with what it is worth on December 31, Somerset is able to see whether his business is growing, shrinking, or remaining stagnant. Clearly his business is growing since his capital grew from $17,785 to $23,430.

WHAT IF THINGS GO POORLY?

How do you know when it's not working out? Let's say things went badly. PBS didn't show its iguana special and no one bought our newsletter. Instead of picking up more subscriptions after July, things carried on sluggishly. By October it looked as though we were only going to pick up ninety subscribers for the whole year.

We would have sat down together, ready to make some serious decisions. Basically, we would need to decide whether to cut our losses or carry on. If we decided to carry on, we would need to do some major rethinking. The reasons for the lack of response could have been false assumptions we made way back in our market research. Perhaps there just aren't as many iguana owners in the United States as we thought. Perhaps the topic is too specialized and our newsletter should be about all reptiles. We would also look at how we ran the business. Is there any way to cut down expenses? And would that be enough? What would happen if we sent the newsletter out by bulk mail, omitting any topical references, so it didn't matter if it arrived late? Should we carry advertising? Perhaps the pricing is wrong: We could be charging too much or too little.

To fix any of these takes time, which would require more money. Now, there might be some working capital left, but we must remember that's going to be needed for the day-to-day running of the business as we keep it going longer and race to meet the new, pushed-back break-even point. To reorganize we'd need another loan. We may have some luck at a bank since we've been in business for a while. More likely we'd go back to our original investors and ask them for more money.

And this is where we would need to be careful. When do we stop? Let's examine that question. If we cut our losses and decide to give up at this point, it doesn't mean we aren't entrepreneurs. It does mean our idea was flawed or badly planned. We just simply made mistakes. Nobody likes to admit he or she made a mistake, but sometimes it's better to swallow your pride and call it quits. If you think your business is heading into trouble, sit down and think about your life during the time you've been running the business. Has it been more fun than when you were in an office? Have you felt more fulfilled? Talk about it with your spouse. How does he or she feel? Would you feel relieved if you could go back to your old job? If you decide that you want to revamp the business and start again, then make sure you feel confident enough again to convince potential investors. Give yourself a deadline by which to turn things around. And stick to that deadline. The good news is that if you do get through a tough period, then you'll be prepared for anything. The flip side is, if you carry on and get deeper and deeper into debt, then it'll take you many years to pay back your debts working at your old day job.

Accounting is a matter of being exact about approximate and fleeting figures. You must constantly monitor your company's health and then constantly readjust your figures. The more you examine and probe, the more trials you do, the fewer errors you'll make. In this chapter we've shown you a few simple ways of judging how well you're running your business. Just remember that, like learning to do tricks with a yo-yo, owning a company is hard work, but if you get the basics right and concentrate, it can be a lot of fun.

The next chapter assumes things have been going well for you and gives you some ideas about what you should do once you break even and start to make a real profit.

For more information on the topics covered in Chapter Fifteen, take a look at the following books:

- *Action Letters for Small Business Owners,* by Wilbur Cross (Wiley, 1991)
- *Cash Flow Letter Book for the Small Business,* by Thomas Morton (Wiley, 1993)
- *Extending Credit & Collecting Cash,* by Lynn Harrison (Crisp, 1993)
- *Financial Letters for the Small Business,* by Thomas Morton (Wiley, 1992)
- *Practical Bookkeeping for the Small Business,* by Mary L. Dyer (Contemporary, 1976)
- *Small-Time Operator: How to Start Your Own Small Business, Keep Your Books, Pay Your Taxes, & Stay Out of Trouble,* by Bernard Kamoroff (Bell Springs, 1993)
- *The Best System: Basic Recordkeeping for a Small Business,* by Thomas P. Duffy (Challenge, 1984)
- *Tools to Help Small Business Improve Their Operations* (Gordon, 1992)

PLANNING YOUR GROWTH

What Happens After You Break Even?

When it looks as though you're going to break even, it's time to start planning the second phase of your business. After all, the point of running a business is not merely to break even, but to actually make a profit.

This chapter will show you how to take a longer view and decide what you want your business to look like in three, five, or even ten years' time. The only requisite for success is growth. You must always be growing in some way. This doesn't necessarily mean your business will be expanding. It will be right-sizing; it will be changing to its most effective size. It's very important that this growth be planned. Too many businesses have begun well and suddenly veered out of control when they tried to move beyond the first year of their financial projections. Either their owners became too ambitious or they tried to play it too safe. The secret is controlled growth that's financed carefully. Even though you've only just broken even, you must plan ahead.

To begin with, you must consider some questions about the direction you want your company to go in. You need to find out whether you want to stay with the business you began or move on to something else. Next you'll need to examine which way you want your company to grow. There are many choices, all with advantages and disadvantages. (In the next chapter we'll talk about financing your decisions.)

WHY YOU MIGHT LEAVE

In Chapter Three, when we examined the attributes that make up the 21st Century entrepreneur, we were concentrating on abilities that could get a business off the ground. Essentially, your role has changed; your job is to keep things going smoothly. It's not easy work—you must be alert and you're always planning ahead, deciding what slight alterations you want to make. But your role is different and you're not creating the way you were.

It's at this point you must decide whether running the business is what you want to do. Is this the role you were looking for when you were slogging through the financial projections and market research? Were you longing for the day you could be running the business, watching the cash flow, predicting the trends, and working on your marketing? Or, even though you openly cursed it, were you secretly enjoying the planning? Did you get an adrenaline rush from convincing people your idea was going to work and persuading them to invest their money? Are you now secretly bored by the idea of watching your business grow? Don't feel bad if this is the case. In fact, it's better that you realize it now than two years from now. Be honest with yourself, because nothing kills a business faster than an unenthusiastic owner. There are various options open to you if you want to start something new, and we'll look at them later on. Right now let's look at whether or not you want to go on with your business.

This may seem like a strange question; after all, the hardest part is behind you. You've set up your business and you may actually be making some money. Surprisingly, it's at this point that some entrepreneurs do leave their businesses in order to start something new. Why is that? Well, there are two kinds of reasons: financial and emotional. We looked at the financial reasons in the last chapter. Let's look at a couple of emotional reasons.

Routine creeps up on all of us. Suddenly it's Thanksgiving, or you smell the scent of new-mown grass, and you realize a whole year has gone by. You may look back on the year happily and hope you have another year just like it. Or you may dread the idea of another year of the same routine. Everyone has bad days (especially in February, it seems), but if your business life just seems to be one long series of bad days, it means you're burned out. It doesn't necessarily mean your company is failing right now, though it will fail if you continue to be unenthusiastic. The solution to this "burnout" is change. We'll examine your options later.

Another reason that can really shake you up is a major change in your life. Sometimes this shock is a positive thing, like a great job offer that will solve some nagging financial problems and still offer you the flexibility of working for yourself. It may be something as simple as realizing that, after thirty years or so, all your children have moved out of the house and can support themselves. We know more than one set of middle-aged parents who have happily given up a lot of the responsibilities of their companies and gone off on frequent extended vacations because they're finally free of their children. Sometimes the shock will be a sad event, like the death of your spouse or your business partner. The shock will make you reconsider your life and your business. You may throw yourself into the business to rid yourself of a sense of loss. Or you may want to take your life in a different direction, without the business.

Bearing in mind these emotional reasons, you should realize that it's important to seriously evaluate the enjoyment you get from the business every now and again. By "seriously evaluate," we mean talking to your family, looking at your accounts, and thinking hard about how much fun you're having. You might even want to consider any job offers you get. Try to see what you could be earning in a regular job. Decide whether you're leading the life you thought you would lead, and decide if this is the life you want. If you decide to let go of your business, there's no one right time to do it, though somewhere around the break-even point is a good time to initially consider it.

Another good time to evaluate your life is when things are going better than they ever have. If you do this self-analysis when you have reason to be optimistic, you're more likely to admit to yourself what's not right. For example, if you've just landed a big project from a new client and you think you've persuaded someone else to hire you, yet you feel despairing about the business, then you should probably consider handing over the company to someone else. If you reach this conclusion when everything's going well financially, your company will seem even more attractive to a prospective buyer.

Because most service businesses are built on intangibles, they can be hard to sell. In some cases you'll be able to pass on your clients as assets. In other cases, like *RIFP,* you'll have more of a product. Whatever your situation, you'll need a fairly established and successful business before you can sell it. You should have a sophisticated business structure, with employees already in place. More important, you need a proven track record as a successful company. This should be illustrated by a number of repeat customers and financial records that show you've been running at a profit. You yourself must be dispensable; no one wants to buy a company that's going to fall apart when you leave. If you put your business on the market, you'll have been scrutinized completely by your accountant and you'll need to submit to some serious delving by any potential buyers. They may ask whether they can pay you as they go along, rather than in one lump sum. You should also feel free to examine the personal finances of anyone who's serious about buying your business before you let that person look at your company's finances. You don't want just anybody looking through your books. You'll also need to be very careful about public relations with your customers, any suppliers you have, and especially with your work force. No one likes dramatic changes, and employees frequently figure it's better to look for a new employer whom they've chosen rather than work for one whom they have had thrust upon them.

STICKING WITH IT, BUT CHANGING THE BUSINESS

Let's assume you want to stay with your business and help it grow. The first question you need to ask yourself is, "Do I want to make more money now, or attract more customers and make more money later?" Your answer will depend on the type of business you're in, the type of personality you have, and what stage of growth your company is at. A young business needs a solid customer base. It can't afford to go for the quick buck. On the other hand, if you see that the business is going to close down within six months due to reasons beyond your control, then you should try and make as much money as you can, as quickly as possible.

We're touching on a point we mentioned briefly in Chapter Thirteen. What happens if your ability to give each customer personal service starts to be stretched to the limit? After all, it was your attentive and caring personal service that attracted your customers in the first place. You may need to turn some customers away. This is going to call on all your powers of tact, but don't think you're driving away a customer forever if you say you can't help right now.

How can you tell when you're in danger of losing that personal touch and, therefore, the quality that makes your business attractive? Find a customer with whom you have a steady relationship and analyze it. Is it a happy relationship? If so, then work out how many hours you spend in personal or telephone contact each week. Then look at a couple of less successful relationships with customers, relationships that seem to be stagnant. See how much time you spend with each of these customers a week. There should be a fairly high correlation between the amount of time you spend with a client and how happy the two of you are with each other. Just because a client always seems to be complaining and demanding doesn't mean he or she isn't pleased with you. Let's say that you spend about an hour a week with your favorite client and ten minutes a week with your least favorite. You should be aiming towards bringing the stagnant relationships up to at least forty-five minutes a week.

But, you may say, if I spend forty-five minutes a week with every client, I won't have any time to find new clients or do any work. Of course, and that's why you need to expand. The goal of any expansion is to make more money. So you have choices: Either (1) charge your current clients more, (2) take on extra staff, (3) start a new, complementary business, (4) unbundle, or (5) look abroad.

CHARGE MORE MONEY

Charging clients more will be acceptable if your services are worth it. It will also hold off a few new customers and control your growth. Health clubs and some professionals do this all the time. In gyms the initiation and membership fees are set artificially high so they're always able to offer a bargain and have a great deal of flexibility. They keep an eye on the number of people using their facilities every day. If the number falls below a certain level, then they encourage people to join by lowering the prices. If they have enough people coming in, then they keep the prices high.

You should also consider what is known as *value billing*. The logic behind value billing is impeccable: If two hours of your expertise and knowledge directly earns your client $230,000, you should obviously charge more than your customary hourly fee. In fact, you should charge your hourly fee plus some previously agreed upon percentage of the final profit or revenues. Make this percentage whatever you think is appropriate. For instance, 1.6 percent is a convincingly precise number!

HIRE MORE PEOPLE

Another way to expand is to hire more people. Refer back to Chapter Fourteen to see the advantages of hiring independent contractors instead of actual employees. But remember, you can't always use independent contractors. A lot of how you'll decide to hire (independent contractor or employee) will depend on the nature of your business. Whatever you choose, you should be aiming to create mini-replicas of yourself: people with a commitment to the company and an eagerness to look after the customers.

One problem is, how much will these "clones" be able to charge? If you are paying them a wage, then there's a rule of thumb that will help you: Employees should bring in three times their "cost." Cost is the wage added to the benefits and your Social Security contributions. These extra costs usually add up to somewhere between a sixth and a third of the wage, depending on the health benefits you're offering. Let's look at a fictional example: Todd Smith runs a small law office and is taking on a new employee, Marnie Connery. Smith is going to pay Connery $330 a week. That means about $100 in Social Security contributions and health benefits, for a total cost of $430 a week. Therefore, Connery must bring in three times $430 every week; that is, $1,290. Assuming Connery works 40 hours a week to make that $1,290, then for one hour she should charge $1,290 ÷ 40, or $32.

At *RIFP,* the phone service we're planning for the second year is the only real personal contact with our customers, unless we meet them at a trade show or special promotion. If we continue to make money, we're going to hire someone to do some of the paperwork and basic bookkeeping for us. What having another person will do is increase the amount of time we're able to spend on the phone with our customers.

Of course, this option may not be feasible for you. If you're a dentist, then people come to see you because of your reputation. They don't want to see your partner, because they don't feel you can transfer your consummate skill to a colleague. Similarly, people who hire a lawyer expect to be able to call and talk to that lawyer, not a junior associate.

ADAPT YOUR BUSINESS

Another option is to keep your original business going along steadily but do something else to complement it. Again you're probably going to need to hire people, but they may be more enthusiastic about starting something from scratch than merely taking over from you. Another advantage is that you retain the tight control of a small business rather than feeling it's expanding and becoming flabby. Often a small business survives by filling a small niche in the market. There's no room or reason for it to grow any bigger. The solution is to find a similar niche and fill it using the expertise you've learned in the first business. Use the original business as a greenhouse, sheltering the new company until it's ready to be transplanted into its own garden.

Elysa Lazar began *The S&B Report* because she noticed an unfilled niche in a market. There were these semisecret warehouse sales all over New York City where clothing manufacturers unloaded their sample clothes at a great discount. She figured rightly that people would pay to know about them. After she started and had gotten to know the market better, she observed that there were similar bargains she could give people information about. Since then, she's started up a number of other services. *Shop by*

Mail is published twice a year and lists manufacturers, discounters, and stores where you can shop cheaply by mail or phone. *The Outlet Report* comes out once a year and describes all the outlet stores around the country, telling you the times they're open and how to get there. By finding niches and filling them, Lazar has managed to carve out more than one profitable business.

You might also follow the example of weight reduction centers and offer a product that fits into your service. While they offer a genuine service—helping people reduce their weight—a great deal of their revenue comes from selling special prepackaged meals. Since their classes are tied to this special diet, there's a built-in market.

UNBUNDLE

Yet another way of expanding is to unbundle. You do this by taking everything you've worked on, that bundle of techniques and pieces of knowledge you've learned, and teaching them to other people. You choose the one thing you do best and put your energy into it. You'll also have the role of general manager, but you won't be involved in every little aspect of your business as you were in the past.

If you got into the business of teaching computer programs because you loved watching others become as excited by them as you, then take yourself out of the office and stick to the classroom, leaving the bookkeeping to your employees. Of course, you'll keep an eye on the finances, but you'll do more for your company's health by being out there in the classroom encouraging good word of mouth than you would by sweating over a calculator in the office.

What you're doing is letting the company breathe a little. Wonderful as you are, after a while the company will take on a life of its own, and you'd be better off surveying the whole thing from a distance. It's a paradox: The very things that made your company a success—your determination and pigheadedness—can rapidly become a problem. You won't see them on your balance sheet under liabilities, but they'll soon start to affect your bottom line. As Karen Bacon's event-planning business grew larger, she had to make changes. "Over the years I've realized how much I need others to make it happen. I used to be superindependent. Now I'm more happy trusting other people. All my work is very collaborative. I rely on the artists, the choreographer, the set designer, and the musicians."

Of course, unbundling is hard to do. But to succeed in your unbundling, you'll either be employing people who are specialists and probably know as much as, if not more than, you, about a subject, or you'll need to teach them the basics and then let them learn the rest on their own. That's the hardest thing to do, but it's essential.

GO GLOBAL

As a 21st Century entrepreneur, you may be looking abroad to clone or adapt your business in a completely fresh market. To some extent you must: If you don't look outwards, you won't see the competition coming in. Look what happened to General Motors when it felt it had an unbeatable product and didn't need to worry about imports. We know what you're thinking. "All the time these two are spending with their iguanas has driven them crazy." They've taking to comparing my little service business to General Motors. While we readily admit to being slightly off center, we're not crazy talking about taking your business global. Just hear us out for a couple of paragraphs.

When most people think of international trade, they think of products being shipped in and out of the country. But remember that where there are businesses, there are business services. There will always be retailers who have more money than you and less information. They need a guiding hand to break into new markets. If you know the market or, better yet, how to cut through the red tape at either end of the import/export shuffle, then you're in a position to command premium fees. Remember that in the 21st Century, information is power, and that if knowledge passes from one company to another through your business, you can charge a fee for this service. And don't forget that international trade is a two-way street. You could be marketing yourself to companies that also want to export to the United States.

Another important source of business is the fact that American culture has become the culture of "youth" all over the world. By the 21st Century, these youths will have grown up, and while we can assume they will begin to value their own cultures more than they did as children, their whole outlook on life will have been influenced by America. Any time you travel abroad, you'll realize that there exists an unlimited desire to be part of the American Dream. We once walked into an English pub and were talking excitedly at the bar about what local ale we were going to try. When the bartender heard our accents, he came over and proudly recommended that we should try this great American beer that he carried called . . . Budweiser.

People new to capitalism (and to an extent, this applies to some of the more socialist countries in the European Community, like Britain and Italy, as well as Central Europe) don't quite get the game. They don't realize that what makes capitalism work is people saying, "I can do it," then starting businesses and plugging away until they're successful; should these ventures fail, they try again. That's why one of the best opportunities for doing business in the 21st Century is in Central Europe: You can teach people how to become capitalists. You'll find plenty of willing students. They need to know how to put together a business team, write a business plan, do market research, create an image, and finance themselves (all things you know well, having done them yourself). And that's before they even start business. Once they're up and running, there's plenty for native-born capitalists to advise upon.

It's important to be aware of the social customs and underlying attitudes of different countries. For example, both the Japanese and the Americans recognize that competition exists in nature and business. However, the Japanese consider harmony the goal of any conflict, whereas the Americans just want to win. Because of this, one thing you're going to need is the ability to wait, watch, listen, and learn. Always go through the "proper" channels with any company you have dealings with. What is considered "daring, innovative" behavior here may well be construed as "foolish, meddlesome" behavior in Japan, unless it has been given thorough consideration by the whole management team.

Joint ventures can be tremendously useful ways to get a foot in the door of any new country or market. You pool your skills or expertise with a like-minded company from your target country, which means both of you profit. There are some important fundamentals to deal with before you even think about signing a contract with another company, however. Examine your future partners' management style—can you live with it? Can they live with yours? What exactly are you getting that you couldn't get on your own, given a little time and effort? Joint ventures are no shortcut to profits. How much control will you have? Often you'll find that certain countries will allow you only 49 percent ownership of a business. Don't underplay the fact that you're handing over the keys to America. In the 21st Century the almighty dollar is worth a lot more than its exchange value: It holds the promise of untold future opportunities. Get your lawyers to check your future partners inside out and back to front. Your unfamiliarity with another culture (be it Polish or Malaysian) means that you won't be able to spot duplicity as easily as you could in the United States.

We can't take you through all the decisions in this chapter in a step-by-step way. Small service businesses have many characteristics in common when they start up, but they develop differently, which means that we can't do more than give you general advice. You will have to examine your own business and decide for yourself whether you want to leave or stay. If you want to stay, as you'll probably have to, given the difficulties of selling a service business, then you must decide how you want to change your business. Remember that it *must* evolve in order to survive. Our next chapter will give you some ideas on how you can go about financing this change.

For more information on the topics covered in Chapter Sixteen, take a look at the following books:

- *Small Business & Venture Capital,* by Rudolph L. Weissman (Ayer, 1979)
- *The Growth Challenge,* by Stephen A. Stumpf (Dearborn, 1993)

❧ 17 ❧

MAINTAINING YOUR CHANGING BUSINESS

How to Finance Expansion

Your business mostly needs one thing to survive and prosper: money. Your personality can give it a good start, and a good market niche is fertile ground in which to grow, but without regular showers of money, nothing spectacular is going to happen. In the last chapter we looked at some of your options for expansion. This chapter will tell you how to bring your plans to life.

Essentially you have two choices; each of them relies on a close reading of your financial information. You can either expand using your profits and cash flow, which is called *bootstrapping,* or you can get refinanced.

BOOTSTRAPPING

"Pulling yourself up by your bootstraps" means doing it on your own, and so bootstrapping has come to describe the process by which a business grows without any outside help. Some businesses do manage to expand this way. By controlling their profits carefully, by taking no risks, and by expanding very slowly, they succeed.

The attraction of financing your expansion this way is the perceived lack of risk. You feel you took a leap of faith when you started up, and now you can sit back and wait for the money to roll in. Well, it might work like that, or it might not. Unfortunately, doing a little for a small business can be just as dangerous as

225

doing a lot. Your small size means you're more vulnerable to being wiped out by any major economic shift; it wouldn't even need to be as big as the recent recession. Even just losing your two major customers could ruin you. That's why you must seriously consider more detailed and larger refinancing, even if you ultimately reject it.

REFINANCING

Your investors, the people who lent you the original money to start up your business, are probably delighted that you're profitable because it means at some point they're going to get their money back. However, unless your profits are incredibly large, these people probably won't be interested in investing any more money. If you're doing very well, you can offer them their money back or see if they want to increase their stakes. Chances are they're going to think they've done their bit as friends and relatives and they'll want to take their money, thank you very much. That's why the best way to refinance is generally through the more conventional routes that weren't open to you when you were starting your business. Now that you have some kind of track record, you can at least show people in the financial world your real figures, not just projections and optimism.

There are two kinds of financing for this second stage of your business: equity or debt. Equity means you promise your investors some of the profits in return for the money they've give you. Debt means you promise your investors you'll pay back their money with interest by a certain time. In other words, you either take on "partners" or borrow the money.

EQUITY FINANCING

Let's look at a couple of the ways to obtain equity financing:

GOING PUBLIC

If you are incorporated, this is an obvious option for your business. Stock is probably one of the reasons you became incorporated in the first place. Selling stock is a complicated and costly business, which will involve a lot of your lawyer's and accountant's time. You've also got to come to grips with the possibility of giving up a lot of the control of your business. This is why selling stock is something that owners consider only when a business is well under way and they're ready to move away from the heart of the company and relax a little.

Shares can be offered as private stock to a specific group of people or they can be offered to the public. In the second case, the entire world gets to have a look at what you're trying to sell. Unsurprisingly, most small businesses tend to go for private placements. These aren't as complicated legally and can be done a little faster.

If you sell stocks to the public, you'll become responsible for the financial well-being of your stockholders. You'll be dealing with a board of directors and stockholder meetings. Entrepreneurs say there's a thrill to be had seeing your company traded on the stock market, but they also describe a deep frustration at being held responsible to stockholders.

What about selling stock informally to friends and family? Well, this is up to you. You can offer them a percentage of your profits the way you'd offer a real stockholder a dividend. This can lead to tension, since they'll hold you responsible if they lose money: You must make sure they understand that, in a bad year, 10 percent of nothing is nothing. You'll need to put your agreement down in writing and discuss it with your accountant and lawyer. You should realize that your stockholders are becoming partners of a sort, and so you'll need to take their opinions into consideration.

Venture Capitalists and Small Business Investment Companies

Small Business Investment Companies (SBICs) are venture capitalists licensed by the SBA. They actually get some of their cash from the SBA, and we can consider them a variation of venture capitalists. We dismissed venture capitalists earlier in the book as hopeless sources for start-up capital. They may be a little more friendly towards you now, as long as you're making decent profits. They'll come in like nosy partners, full of advice and demands. And you must be sure that they're interested in long-term profits, and are not just looking for a quick return. Once the business is doing well, they may also want you to buy back a large part of their stock in the company at a predetermined profit. This is called a "put." They may also make you a loan that is convertible into your stock at a predetermined low price. This is called a "call."

Venture capitalists usually divide their investment into part debt and part equity. This means they're not in the hole for too much if you go bust, and they're not left kicking themselves if your business does take off. They are, quite sensibly, trying to balance their risks and rewards.

When looking for either venture capitalists or SBICs, check out their preferences. Some like high-tech businesses, some prefer services, others retail. You also want to make it look as if you could become a large corporation if only you had the opportunity. Basically, all venture capitalists and SBICs are hoping you're going to be another Apple Computer. So try and market yourself as though you might be. For that reason alone, *RIFP* wouldn't be at all attractive to them. But an entire publishing house devoted to newsletters, each newsletter concentrating on different pets and the needs of their owners, might be attractive.

DEBT FINANCING

Equity financing is useful as a long-term tool for expansion. Debt is better for short-term answers to problems. We'll look at some places where you can find some debt financing, but before we do, you'll need to go back to your business checklist to update the figures and reassess your goals. You'll also need to prepare a loan proposal. This will include an income statement, a balance sheet, a projected cash budget for the period of the proposed loan—this should indicate your ability to repay the loan within that period—and an executive summary that describes your man-agement team and the nature of the business. You should work this out carefully with your accountant. Now let's examine the potential recipients of your loan proposal:

COMMERCIAL BANKS

Like venture capitalists, the banks we so readily dismissed in Chapter Eleven may now be more open to the idea of lending you money. They're likely to have the best interest rates and will be used to dealing with cases like yours. Usually they're most interested in a short-term loan of a year or less that will cover some particular expenditure like new equipment or supplies.

Finding the right bank can be tricky, but you probably already have some sort of a relationship with one or two banks, so start there. Ask your professionals whether they can help you find a bank or, more particularly, a bank officer who can help you.

At this stage in your business your bank may be willing to offer you an asset-based loan. The bank lends you money assuming that you are going to collect certain accounts receivable. When you do collect, you pay back the bank, plus interest. The bank uses your assets—trucks, computers—as collateral.

Remember you'll be paying the bank interest, so it will profit by helping you. You're also giving it good word of mouth, by helping it to present itself as a bank that supports the local community.

THE U.S. SMALL BUSINESS ADMINISTRATION

Just as when you were looking for start-up capital, you should consider using the SBA's resources. The process is complicated and time-consuming, but they may be able to help you. The paperwork and waiting lists argue against the SBA being the source of a quick fix of cash, but it can help you out with any longer-term financial plans you have.

COMMERCIAL LENDERS

These may take greater risks than banks. They may also be willing to be more creative in their terms, agreeing to factor in money for accounts receivable. Unfortunately, they balance this risk taking by charging higher interest rates and levying large penalties if you pay off the loan early and rob them of the interest they were expecting.

SUPPLIERS

Go back to your suppliers and see whether they can help you again. They should be pleased they've managed to get a year or so's worth of orders from you. They may allow you to pay bills after sixty, or even ninety, days, which is, in effect, a loan. Phillipe Kahn, founder of the computer software company Borland International, Inc. (a name he made up to sound corporate), had a great method of convincing vendors that his business was doing well. He invited them to see his office. While they were there, they couldn't help but notice how busy the phones were with people placing orders, and they left convinced he was a good risk. Only they didn't know the staff and the phone calls were fakes, pulled together to impress them. We're not recommending you try something as audacious as this, but don't be afraid to promote yourself.

LEASING

If the money you need is going towards buying new equipment, then, as we suggested before, see if you can lease the equipment instead. This way you avoid a scary lump-sum bill for a new photocopier. Often you'll also get servicing thrown in free. You might even find places where you can lease with an option to buy.

After looking at all these choices, you might ask yourself, "When am I supposed to find the time to do business?" It's a legitimate question. Part of the answer is that you won't. By now you should have delegated many of your business responsibilities to other people, people who are as qualified and as enthusiastic as you. You should be able to look up from your desk and see your business, mentally and visually. You should have a good idea of what everyone working for you is doing. Most of all, you should feel very proud. You're looking at your own creation. And your creation, while shaped by the world around it, has triumphed over obstacles and negativity. You are helping to shape the America of the 21st Century.

For more information on the topics covered in Chapter Seventeen, take a look at the following books:

- *Small Business & Venture Capital,* by Rudolph L. Weissman (Ayer, 1979)
- *The Growth Challenge,* by Stephen A. Stumpf (Dearborn, 1993)

~&~ **APPENDIX A** ~&~

Here's how you will gradually discover your business idea.
Keep track of your progress with the date spaces on the right.

Chapter	Task	Date Begun	Date Completed
4	Soak up what society finds important	_____	_____
4	Write down EVERYTHING that interests you	_____	_____
4	Find "fields" by grouping together similar ideas	_____	_____
4	Ask common-sense questions about each field	_____	_____
4	List the fields according to (a) what you want to do most and (b) what you can do best.	_____	_____
4	Choose the 3 or 4 fields that are at the top of both lists	_____	_____

Chapter	Task	Date Begun	Date Completed
5	Research each field in depth	_____	_____
5	Write down all your business ideas; sleep; pick your favorite	_____	_____
6	Ask yourself 8 questions about your idea	_____	_____
6	Talk to your family	_____	_____
6	Ask potential clients questions	_____	_____
6	Ask potential rivals questions	_____	_____

☜ APPENDIX B ☞

This appendix lays out the steps you'll take before you make the leap and actually open for business.

Chapter	Task	Date Begun	Date Completed
7	Choosing your company name	_____	_____
7	Choosing your company philosophy	_____	_____
8	Choosing location	_____	_____
9	Calculating start-up costs	_____	_____
10	Calculating fees	_____	_____
10	Calculating working capital	_____	_____
11	Finding seed money	_____	_____
12	Getting your clients' attention	_____	
13	Keeping your client's attention	_____	
14	Finding people to work for you	_____	_____

⇜ APPENDIX C ⇝

This appendix will help you keep track of what you've done as you calculate your working capital.

Task	Date Begun	Date Completed
(1) Estimate monthly fixed costs: rent, salary, utilities, advertising, etc.	_____	_____
(2) Estimate monthly variable costs: supplies, others' salaries, etc.	_____	_____
(3) Estimate your fees according to your billable hours per week.	_____	_____
(4) Work out when the fees will allow you to break even.	_____	_____
(5) Calculate working capital—i.e., the money needed to keep your business afloat until you've broken even.	_____	_____

≪ APPENDIX D ≫

Month-by-Month Profit-and-Loss Statement for Your Business

	Jan.	Feb.	March
Sales revenue:	$	$	$
Cash inflow:	$	$	$
Less costs[1]:	$	$	$
Net income before taxes:	$	$	$

	April	May	June
Sales revenue:	$	$	$
Cash inflow:	$	$	$
Less costs:	$	$	$
Net income before taxes:	$	$	$

	July	Aug.	Sept.
Sales revenue:	$	$	$
Cash inflow:	$	$	$
Less costs:	$	$	$
Net income before taxes:	$	$	$

	Oct.	Nov.	Dec.
Sales revenue:	$	$	$
Cash inflow:	$	$	$
Less costs:	$	$	$
Net income before taxes:	$	$	$

[1] Variable + fixed costs from Chapter Ten.

❧ APPENDIX E ❧

A Blank Balance Sheet
for You to Use

YOUR COMPANY
Balance Sheet
December 31, 199—

Assets

Current assets
    Cash on hand $
    Cash in bank $
    Accounts receivable $
    Merchandise inventory $
    Supplies $
    Prepaid rent $
        Total current assets $ _____

Plant and equipment
    Equipment $
    Less accumulated   −
      depreciation
        Total plant and
           equipment $ _____
        Total assets $ _____

Liabilities and Owner's Equity

Current liabilities:

    Accounts payable $

    Note payable to bank $

    Income taxes payable $

        Total current

          liabilities $_____

Owner's equity:

Your name, capital, Jan 1, $

  199—

Add net income for the year   +_____

Less withdrawals by the

  owner $_____

Your name, capital,

  Dec 31, 199— $_____

Total liabilities and owner's

  equity $_____

✧ INDEX ✧